This is
Citizenship 3

Julia Fiehn Terry Fiehn

This is
Citizenship 3

Julia Fiehn Terry Fiehn

Hachette UK's policy is to use papers that are natural, renewable and recyclable products and made from wood grown in sustainable forests. The logging and manufacturing processes are expected to conform to the environmental regulations of the country of origin.

Orders: please contact Bookpoint Ltd, 130 Milton Park, Abingdon, Oxon OX14 4SB. Telephone: (44) 01235 827720. Fax: (44) 01235 400454. Lines are open 9.00–5.00, Monday to Saturday, with a 24-hour message answering service. Visit our website at www.hoddereducation.co.uk.

© Terry Fiehn, Julia Fiehn 2010
First published in 2010 by
Hodder Education,
An Hachette UK company
338 Euston Road
London NW1 3BH

Impression number   5 4 3 2 1
Year   2014 2013 2012 2011 2010

Cover photo: © Gary Jochim/Superstock
Illustrations by Chris Rothero/Linden Artists, Janek Matysiak, Karen Donnelly, Oxford Designers & Illustrators and Tony Randell
Designed by Lorraine Inglis Design in Frutiger Roman 11/14pt
Printed in Italy

A catalogue record for this title is available from the British Library.

ISBN: 978 0340 947 159

Titles in the series
This is Citizenship 1 Pupil's Book 978 0340 947 098
This is Citizenship 1 Teacher's Resource 978 0340 947 104
This is Citizenship 1 Dynamic Learning 978 0340 947 111

This is Citizenship 2 Pupil's Book 978 0340 947 128
This is Citizenship 2 Teacher's Resource 978 0340 947 135
This is Citizenship 2 Dynamic Learning 978 0340 947 142

This is Citizenship 3 Pupil's Book 978 0340 947 159
This is Citizenship 3 Teacher's Resource 978 0340 947 166
This is Citizenship 3 Dynamic Learning 978 0340 947 173

Contents

The Publishers would like to thank the following for permission to reproduce copyright material:

Photo credits
p.7 © Alex Wong/Getty Images; **p.8** © Ana Ortegan/Amnesty International; **p.14** © Eddie Mulholland/Rex Features; **p.15** © Rex Features; **p.19** © Etienne Ansotte/ Rex Features; **p.29** © Feng Li/Getty Images; **p.36** logos by permission of Animals Count, Conservative Party, DUP, Green Party, Labour Party, Liberal Democrats, Libertarian Party, National Liberal Party, Official Monster Raving Loony Party, Plaid Cymru, Respect Party, SDLP, Sinn Fein, SNP, UKIP, UUP; **p.52** logos by permission of Age Concern and Help the Aged, Amnesty International UK, ASH, CND, Countryside Alliance, Fathers4Justice, Greenpeace UK, The Law Society, Liberty, NSPCC, Plane Stupid, RHA; **p.54** logos by permission of Animal Liberation Front, PETA, RSPCA, r © PETA, reproduced with permission; **p.62** A, C & D © Rex Features, B ©Photodisc/Getty Images; **p.63** E, G & J © Rex Features, F ©Tim Rooke/ Rex Features, H © BBC, I © Pool/Getty Images; **p.68** logos by permission of RHA, Plane Stupid and CND; **p.71** t © Rex Features, b ©Tony Kyriacou/Rex Features; **p.72** t © volki – Fotolia.com, cl & bl ©Photodisc/Getty Images, cr ©Sven Creutzmann/ Mambo photo/Getty Images, br © broker – Fotolia.com; **p.79** © Phil Yeomans/ BNPS; **p.82** t ©National Pictures/TopFoto, b Reproduced with kind permission of the Commonwealth Secretariat; **p.83** © EMMANUEL DUNAND/AFP/Getty Images; **p.84** tr UN Photo/John Isaac, tl UN Photo/Eskinder Debebe, tc © FARZANA WAHIDY/ AFP/Getty Images, cl © Abid Katib/Getty Images, cr © SAYYID AZIM/AP/Press Association Images, bl WHO/P. Virot, br UN Photo/Logan Abassi; **p.86** t © Kevin Weaver/Rex Features, b © Action Press/Rex Features; **p.88** © Per-Anders Pettersson/ Getty Images; **p.89** © Patrick Frilet/Rex Features; **p.92** c UN Photo/John Isaac, r Reproduced with kind permission of the Commonwealth Secretariat.

Acknowledgements
p.14 article extract from 'Two wheels: good. Two legs: terrorist suspect' © *Times Newspapers Ltd*; **p.15** extract on anti-terrorism laws © *Independent News and Media Limited*; **p.19** extracts from www.ico.gov.uk/Youth/section2/other_peoples_ stories.aspx (Information Commissioners Office), *Derby Evening Telegraph* extract © *Derby Telegraph Media Group Ltd*; **p.29** article on Eleanor Simmons from www.pinkstinks.co.uk/pdfs/10.pdf, by permission of Abi & Emma Moore; **p.77** 'EU ban on knobbly fruit and veg to be "re-peeled"' extract from the *Daily Express*, 12 November 2008, Copyright © Northern and Shell Media Publications, extract from 'Prison sentences for picking wild flowers under EU green laws' from the *Daily Mail*, 7 February 2007, by permission of Solo Syndication Ltd, extract from 'Headlights on in day, says EU' from *The Sun*, 11 October 2006, © News Group Newspapers Ltd; **p.79** extract from 'EU bans pets from farm B&B' from the *Daily Mail*, 12 June 2008, by permission of Solo Syndication Ltd.

People living in the UK expect their rights to be protected. There is a long history in this country of people fighting for different rights such as the right to vote, the right to own property, the right to a fair trial, the right to express an opinion and the right to protest against government decisions. In some countries in the world today, people have very few rights and they can be imprisoned without a trial, and then tortured, or even killed, especially if they disagree with the Government.

Having rights and living in a free society leads some people to think that they can behave exactly as they wish. But if they do, they may affect other people's rights. If we are all to get along together, people need to behave responsibly towards one another, even if they don't always agree.

KEY WORDS
civil liberties

human rights

surveillance

privacy

discrimination

prejudice

equal opportunities

Assessing your progress

In this section you will be assessing how well you can:

- explain and justify your opinion, giving some evidence
- decide how rights need to be balanced
- negotiate between different points of view
- understand why other people have different points of view
- understand that in the UK people's rights are protected
- understand that people may claim conflicting rights.

1.1 Human rights and civil liberties – right or wrong?

People have different kinds of rights. Human rights are basic rights that everyone is entitled to expect and that all human beings should have, no matter where in the world they live. Examples are the right to life, freedom from torture and freedom from slavery.

Free countries support human rights. They also have other laws, which are not always the same as human rights, to protect people from any abuse of power by the government of that country. These rights are called **civil liberties**. Not all free countries have the same civil liberties. For example, in the USA, people see the right to carry guns, or 'bear arms' as a civil liberty, but this is not the case in the UK, where there are strict laws controlling who is allowed to carry a gun.

Living in a society where rights are guaranteed leads some people to think they have the right to behave exactly as they wish, even though their behaviour might offend or inconvenience other people. We need to think about how to balance one person's rights against another person's. The law tries to protect everyone's rights, but sometimes there is disagreement. For example, the debate about whether or not people should be allowed to smoke in public led to a law forbidding it.

A
Fred Jones and his wife have twin toddlers. They love to take the twins out on Saturdays to eat in a restaurant in the town centre. They believe they have a right to take the children wherever they go. Sometimes the twins argue and fight, run about and make a noise in the restaurant. Other customers complain that they have the right to a peaceful meal.

Activity

1 In pairs, look at the following situations. Decide whether you agree with each person.
2 When you have decided which people you agree with, join up with another pair and see if you all feel the same way.
3 Choose two situations where you think the person has a good case and decide what should happen. Your teacher can tell you the legal position in each situation.

B
Jo Cheung is a keen supporter of animal rights. She intends to demonstrate in a big rally that has been planned outside a research laboratory. The police have decided to cancel the rally because of threats of violence and risks to the safety of workers at the laboratory. Jo says her rights to make her views known have been denied by the police.

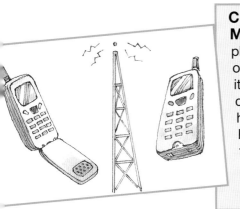

C

Mehmit Ali is worried that a mobile phone mast is about to be erected on the building next door. He thinks it will be a hazard to the health of his children and says that his right to a healthy environment will be affected. However, the phone company says that there must be more masts if mobile phone users are to be able to get a signal to use their phones.

D

Jane Simpson has written a magazine article about people who come from a particular country. It is a very critical article and says some very unpleasant things. The editor of the magazine says he will not publish the article because it would offend people. Jane argues that she has a right to freedom of expression, to say what she believes to be the truth.

E
Harry Tanner
has a large, noisy dog. It barks all the time, night and day. Harry says it keeps burglars away and he loves it very much. It is his companion. The neighbours can take no more of the barking and say they have the right to sleep at night. They are demanding that he either moves or gets rid of the dog. Harry says he has a right to keep it.

G

Rob Ross loves music and likes to listen to it wherever he is. He has a mobile phone that plays music and sometimes he wants to listen to it out loud and not just through earphones. One day when he is listening to his music on the bus, a woman in the seat behind says that she does not want to hear his music and would prefer him to use his earphones.

F

Maroula Mitchell has found out that her employer has been monitoring her emails to her boyfriend from the company computer. The employer says she is wasting time at work, which he is paying her for, but Maroula says she has a right to privacy and to communicate with friends if she wishes.

Developing your negotiation skills

Negotiation skills are necessary in everyday life and the aim of negotiation is to produce a 'win-win' situation – in other words, no one feels they have lost. The best negotiators try to get what they want by finding a solution on which both sides can agree.

Activity

1 Work in threes. Role play the three situations A–C from pages 2–3. Two of you take the roles of the people who disagree about their rights, and the other person is the observer. Rotate the roles in each new situation, so everyone gets a chance to be the observer. During each role play, the two who disagree must follow the tips for negotiators and see whether they come to some agreement. The observer must watch and listen carefully and write notes on how well the other two negotiated.

2 Choose one of the other situations D–G from pages 2–3, and try negotiating without any role cards to help you.

3 Each group of three should join another group to make groups of six. Discuss how the negotiations went and whether solutions were found. What worked best? What didn't work?

Tips for negotiators

- Be clear in your own mind of the outcome that you would like, but be prepared to make compromises.

- Listen carefully to what the other person is saying and don't interrupt and argue.

- Explain your own position calmly and politely.

- Summarise what you think the other person's view is, to make sure that you understand it. Ask them if you have got it right.

- Keep looking for compromises that you could agree with.

- Think about the consequences of any compromises.

- Keep notes if the negotiation is complicated.

- Always stay cool and polite.

Situation A: Role card for Fred/Fred's wife

You have twin boys who are lively little chaps. They are very sociable and love to come out with you when you go to restaurants, and also to friends' houses and sometimes the cinema. They don't settle well with babysitters, and you are reluctant to leave them. However, you just couldn't bear to stay at home every weekend, and believe that you have a right to go out with the boys. It's true that they won't sit still, and sometimes get a bit whiney because they are tired. However, when you go abroad, there are always children in the restaurants, and you think that people in this country are very anti-children. They should be more tolerant.

Situation A: Role card for another diner in the restaurant

You are part of a retired couple who are not very well-off. When you go out for a meal, it is a special treat. You have two grown-up children, who now have children of their own. You get really annoyed when you find that your evening is spoiled by over-tired and restless children, who cannot be expected to sit quietly in a restaurant, but whose noise stops you being able to relax and chat over the food. When your children were little, you got a babysitter for them. As they got older you sometimes took them out to restaurants, but if they misbehaved, you took them outside. You just can't understand why young parents are so inconsiderate.

Situation B: Role card for Jo Cheung

You are a supporter of animal rights and believe that animals should never be used in experiments, even for medicines. You are keen to take part in a demonstration against animal experiments which are being done in a local laboratory. However, you have been told that the demonstration has been banned by the police because there have been some threats against the safety of people working at the lab. You absolutely do not agree with violence, and would never get involved in that. However, you are very angry that your right to protest has been taken away by the senior police officers, and you think they are abusing their power.

Situation B: Role card for senior police officer

It is your job to protect the public and keep the peace. Usually, you work closely with people who plan demonstrations so that protesters can have their right to voice their opinion. However, this right does not run to committing violence against others. You have been given a tip-off that some of the protesters plan to attack workers at a laboratory which carries out experiments on animals as part of medical research. After some high-level meetings, you decide to ban the demonstration because you think someone will get hurt.

Situation C: Role card for Mehmit Ali/Mehmit's wife

You live next to a tall building and have seen notices on the building announcing that planning permission is being sought for a mobile phone mast to be put on the top. You have young children and have read that there is a suggestion that the signals from masts can have an effect on children's brain development. You are very worried that there could be health risks if the mast is erected and you will oppose the planning permission by writing to the local council and drawing up a petition for local people to sign.

Situation C: Role card for representative of the mobile phone company

Your job in the mobile phone company is to secure sites for new masts. Some customers have been complaining that they cannot get a signal in some parts of town. They have paid good money for their mobile phones and should be able to make and receive calls wherever they are. As far as you are aware, there is no clear evidence that phone masts cause any health problems at all, and you think the protesters, who probably have mobile phones themselves, are selfish not to agree to have a mast near them.

A woman's right to choose?

Some rights are very controversial. They concern deeply held religious or moral values. Abortion is a subject that causes a great deal of disagreement.

Wendy Harrington is ten weeks pregnant. She does not wish to have the child, since she is only seventeen years old and does not want a long-term relationship with the father. She has decided to have an abortion and believes it is a woman's right to choose. However, the father of the child wants her to have the baby and says he will care for it. He feels he has the right to demand that the child be born. Wendy's aunt is religious and is a member of a pro-life group which believes that every foetus has a right to life.

This is a serious debate about rights in conflict. What arguments would the three put forward?

Activity

1 Look at the points below and decide who would use each one on your own copy of this table. One point for each side has been done for you.

Wendy	The father	The aunt (pro-life)
A woman has the right to decide what happens to her own body.	A person shouldn't be denied the right to bring up his own child.	Every person has the right to life and a foetus is a person.

A A foetus is not a person; it is a bundle of cells without feelings or consciousness.

B A woman who does not choose to become pregnant should be able to end the pregnancy.

C God gives life; it is not up to human beings to decide who lives and dies.

D A child can ruin a young woman's career before it has even begun and will determine the rest of her life.

E A foetus is carrying both parents' genes, so it is part of the father as much as the mother.

F A father who is prepared to look after the child should have a say.

G Fathers are supposed to take responsibility for babies, so they have a right to say what happens to the foetus.

H It's the woman who has to carry and bear the child and look after it.

Activity

Debate

2 You have now sorted out some of the main points for and against abortion in this case, although the points are not fully explained.

a) The class should split into three groups. Each group adopts one of the positions from the situation on page 6.

b) Each group should develop the arguments for this position, adding any others they can think of.

c) Hold a debate between the two combined groups who oppose abortion and the one group that supports it. You will need a chairperson. Two people from each side should make the opening statements in the debate. Then everybody else can join in.

DISCUSS

1 After the debate, decide which argument you agree with most. Do other people agree? Has anyone's opinion been changed?

2 Think back over the debate and the situations you looked at in the previous section.

a) Why is it not easy to decide whose rights are the most important in a situation?

b) Do you think there will always be conflicts of rights? Why?

c) How can these best be dealt with?

I It is morally wrong and wicked to kill the foetus.

J It is not a good idea to bring an unwanted child into the world.

K It is irresponsible to run the risk of getting pregnant when you don't want to have a baby – people should not have sex or they should take proper precautions.

The Human Rights Act

The Human Rights Act 1998 came into full force in the UK from 2 October 2000. The rights apply to everyone in the UK, whether or not they are British citizens, and the government must make sure they receive their rights. The rights in the Act are based on the European Convention for the Protection of Human Rights.

The Human Rights Act covers the following areas:

- Everyone has the right to life.

- No one can be tortured or given degrading punishment.

- No one can be held in slavery or forced labour.

- Everyone has the right to liberty and security.

- Anyone accused of a crime is entitled to a fair and public hearing in court.

- No one can be punished for an action which was not a crime when it was committed.

- Everyone has the right to privacy and family life.

- Everyone has the right to freedom of opinions and religion.

- Everyone has the right to freedom of expression.

- Everyone has the right to protest peacefully and to join, or not to join, a trade union.

- Men and women of marriageable age have the right to marry and have a family.

- Everyone has the right to own and enjoy their property.

- No one can be denied the right to an education.

- There must be free elections at regular intervals, with secret voting, so that people can choose their own government.

- No one can be punished with the death penalty.

- No one can be discriminated against, on any grounds, in getting these rights.

Activity

Look at each of the cases on the opposite page and answer these questions.
1 What problems do these people face?
2 Which rights do you think have been denied them?
3 What do you think should happen in each case to resolve the problem?

8

Case 1

A young man has been seriously injured in a rugby accident. He is unable to move any of his limbs and is confined to a wheelchair. He cannot live independently, he finds his life intolerable and has told his parents that he wants to die. It is against the law for any doctor to help him to die, and so he and his parents will travel to a clinic in Switzerland where he will get the help he wants. He believes that he should have the right to be helped to die in his own country, and that this should be a human right.

Case 2

A woman is speeding in her car along a motorway, with two passengers. The car is travelling at 95 miles per hour and is caught on a speed camera. The registration number allows the woman to be traced and she receives a letter asking whether she was the driver of the car on the occasion that it was speeding. She refuses to give the information about who was driving and says that the Human Rights Act allows her privacy, and she should not have to say where she was on that day.

Case 3

A young woman has recently arrived in the country, married to a British citizen. She married him when he met her on holiday and travelled back with him as his wife. She was very glad to escape from her home because her father regularly beat her, but she now regrets the marriage very much. Her new husband treats her like a servant, expects her to do everything in the house and will not allow her to go out. She believes that she is being held in slavery, but is frightened to tell anyone, because she does not know whether she is protected under the Human Rights Act.

Case 4

An ex-prisoner was held in a prison for four years without a flushing toilet in his cell. He was forced to 'slop out' every day (to carry his bucket to the toilet block and empty it there). He claims that this amounted to a degrading punishment under the Human Rights Act, and that the British Government owes him compensation. He intends to go to court.

Case 5

A thirteen-year-old boy has been disruptive at his school ever since he arrived there at the beginning of Year 7. The parents of other pupils in the class have complained that he is preventing their children from making educational progress. The head teacher of the school has decided that the boy should be excluded permanently from the school. No other school in the area is prepared to take him because of his record of misbehaviour, which includes violence towards teachers. His mother says she is going to take up the matter under the Human Rights Act because she thinks he is being denied an education.

The police need powers if they are to do their job of preventing crime and arresting suspects. Many of us are likely to come into contact with the police at some time in our lives, whether as victims of crime, witnesses or suspects. It is important that we are treated properly, whatever the reason for dealings with the police. For this reason there are laws and codes of practice which say how police officers should use their powers when carrying out their duties.

Stop and search

Some young people will experience 'stop and search' on the streets, especially in large cities.

1 The police have the power to stop and search you in the street, or in your vehicle, if they have 'reasonable suspicion' that you are carrying:
   - controlled illegal drugs
   - an offensive weapon
   - stolen goods
   - tools for a burglary or theft
   - alcohol to a sports fixture
   - alcohol or tobacco if you are under-age.

2 'Reasonable suspicion' must be based on your behaviour, and not on the kind of person you are (race, age, nationality and so on), or how you are dressed. However, if the police think you are wearing something to try to hide your identity and that a violent crime might be committed, they can ask you to remove it.

3 Before the search, the police officer should give:
   - proof that he or she is a police officer, by showing a warrant card
   - information on police powers to stop and search and the individual's rights in these circumstances
   - his or her name and police station
   - the grounds for the search
   - how to get hold of a record of the search.

4 The police can ask you to remove outer clothing for a search in the street, but would need to take you to a more private place, such as a police van, if other clothing or shoes are removed. You must be searched by someone of the same sex as you.

5 You can only be forced to go to a police station if you are arrested. You could be arrested if you refuse to co-operate with the police and to give your name and address.

Arrest

1 You should be told why you have been arrested and the police should caution you, as follows:

" You do not have to say anything. But it may harm your defence if you do not mention when questioned something which you later rely on in court. Anything you do say may be given in evidence. "

2 Someone should be told of your arrest and you should be able to see a solicitor, although you do not necessarily have the right to a phone call.

3 You can be held at the police station for 24 hours without charge, but this can be 36 hours for some serious offences. In an extreme case, such as allegations of terrorism, the police can apply to a magistrate to keep someone for up to 72 hours.

Interview and charge

1 If you are under seventeen, an 'appropriate adult' should be present while you are interviewed. This could be a family member, a solicitor or a teacher, for example.

2 The interview will be tape-recorded.

3 After the interview the police may:
- charge you with an offence
- remand you in custody
- release you on police bail
- release you after a formal caution
- release you without charge.

4 If you are charged, the custody officer will read out the charges against you and ask if you have anything to say. You will receive a copy of the charges and a date of the court appearance.

5 You may be finger-printed and photographed. If you refuse to have your fingerprints taken, the police can apply to a magistrate to make you agree.

Activity

1 Work in pairs. Complete a chart like the one below.

	Summary of police powers	Summary of rights of the suspect
stop and search		
arrest		
interview and charge		

2 In your pair decide which of the rights of the suspect is the most important. Explain why.

What advice would you give?

Activity

1 Ali, Jordan, Suzy and Donna are friends of yours. Each of them has come up against the police in the last few weeks. They don't know their rights, and need your help. Read each situation and answer the questions that relate to them.

Suzy had been shopping for clothes in town with Donna. As she left the shop, a security guard and a male police officer approached the two girls. The security guard said that he believed that Suzy had stolen some clothing. The police officer asked her to open her shopping, but Suzy refused. The police officer insisted and said that if she wouldn't let him, he'd have to arrest her and take her to the police station. So Suzy agreed, but when she opened her bags, there was no stolen clothing in there.

Did the police officer have the legal right to search Suzy's bag?

When Suzy's bags were found to be empty, the security guard turned to Donna. He said that she had probably stuffed the stolen clothes up inside her jacket. He asked the police officer to search her then and there, before the two girls tried to run off. The police officer grabbed Donna and took off her jacket, though Donna tried to stop him. There were no stolen goods under the jacket.

Did the police officer have the right to search Donna?

Ali and Jordan were hanging about with some friends on the estate where they live. A fight started between two of the other boys, and one pulled a knife. A neighbour called the police, and all the boys were arrested and taken to the police station. The knife had been dropped on the ground, so the police wanted to take everyone's fingerprints to see who had been holding it. Ali and Jordan allowed their fingerprints to be taken, but were not sure that they had to.

Did the police have the legal right to take Ali's and Jordan's fingerprints?

The police interviewed each of the boys separately. Jordan, who is sixteen, wanted his mum to come to the police station, but she had her mobile turned off and the police couldn't contact her. They decided to interview him on his own because they had interviewed all of the others with their parents and wanted to clear the matter up.

Did the police have the legal right to interview Jordan?

Activity

2 Work in threes. One of you should take on the role of the suspect of a crime, one an arresting officer, and one an observer. Role play a street arrest for a suspected robbery. Both the police officer and the suspect should act responsibly. If either is unreasonable, it could affect their future position in court. The observer should note down any mistakes made by the suspect and by the police officer and should report what has been noted at the end of the role play.

DISCUSS

Do you think the police have sufficient powers to do their job properly? Should they have more powers or fewer?

1.4 Laws on terrorism

Since major terrorism attacks have been committed across the world, the government has passed laws which give the police and courts more powers to try to catch and punish terrorists.

Definition of terrorism

The law defines terrorism as:

" The use or threat of action (i.e. violence or a risk of violence to people or property) designed to influence the government or intimidate the public for the purpose of advancing a political, religious, or ideological cause. "

(summarised from the Terrorism Act 2000)

In 2006, the Act was altered to include new offences:

- encouragement of terrorism
- giving out terrorist publications
- 'glorification' of terrorism
- being a member of a forbidden organisation (such as al-Qaeda or Hamas).

The Terrorism Act allows the police to stop, search and move on anyone present in a particular area, if there is evidence of a real terrorist threat, without having to have 'reasonable grounds'. But some people think that the Terrorism Act takes away the democratic rights of ordinary protesters, or even people who are just going about their everyday business.

Example 1: Sally Cameron

'I've been walking to work every morning for months and months to keep fit. One day, I was told by a guard on the gate that I couldn't use the route any more because it was solely a cycle path and he said, if I was caught doing it again, I'd be arrested ... The next thing I knew, the harbour master had driven up behind me with a megaphone, saying, 'You're trespassing, please turn back'. It was totally ridiculous. I started laughing and kept on walking. Cyclists going past were also laughing ... But then two police cars roared up beside me and cut me off, like a scene from Starsky and Hutch, and officers told me I was being arrested under the Terrorism Act.'

DISCUSS

Consider each example on pages 14–15 and discuss whether you think the police are using the Terrorism Act properly.

Example 2: Alleged terrorists

In June 2007, there were attempted car bomb attacks in central London, and at Glasgow airport. In London, two Mercedes containing petrol, gas cylinders and nails were left in streets near nightspots. The cars failed to explode. The next day, a burning car loaded with gas cylinders was driven at the door of the terminal building at Glasgow airport. Following these events, the police used section 44 of the Terrorism Act to allow them to increase stop and search – more than 350 people a day were stopped and searched in London during the next month. This was a monthly total of 10,948 stops, compared to a monthly average of 2,114. Scotland Yard said the stops were 24 per cent Asian, 15 per cent black and 54 per cent white.

Example 3: Protesters

Police used anti-terrorism laws to arrest five people they suspect of planning to disrupt the G20 summit in London (2009). Three men and two women, who were thought to be political activists, were taken into police custody on Friday after police officers discovered imitation weapons, fireworks and political literature during a search of a flat in Plymouth.

The investigation was sparked after a 25-year-old man was arrested for allegedly spraying graffiti on a wall in Plymouth city centre, prompting officers to carry out a search of his flat. There they discovered a number of suspicious items including a replica Kalashnikov assault rifle and several minor explosive devices made from fireworks.

Activity

1 Read the arguments below and decide which ones you agree with.
2 Which ones are in favour of the police having more powers, and which ones are against them having more powers?

A Terrorism calls for extreme measures to fight it. The police must be able to prevent terrorism before it happens, to save lives.

B Our freedoms should not be taken away because of the threat of terrorism. That way, the terrorists have won.

C Terrorists should be caught and treated like any other criminals, using fair laws that protect everyone's rights, and not assuming people are guilty without evidence.

D We should not mind the police being careful and stopping us if they are suspicious. If we are innocent, we have nothing to fear.

The police used the controversial 'kettling' technique to keep the protesters penned in

E If the police have greater powers, they might use these against ordinary people who are perfectly innocent, but a nuisance to the police, like protesters.

F We must trust the Government, the police and the security services to know what is best for us. They have probably got information that we don't know about.

The surveillance society

It is now possible to track ordinary people as they go about their everyday lives. Technology is making it easier all the time for the authorities to pinpoint where people are and what they are doing. Also, the government, the police and big companies hold a lot of information on us; and often we give away information about ourselves on internet social networking sites. Some people say all this is a threat to our privacy and our civil liberties.

Mobile phones

Sophisticated devices can listen in to mobile phone conversations. Even when the phone is on stand-by, it is in contact with the base station, telling it where you and the phone are. Phones with GPS can even tell others what kinds of shops, restaurants, clubs or places of worship you are visiting.

Credit and debit cards

Paying by card shows where you have been and what you have bought. Taking cash out of a bank machine provides a record of where that card has been used and how much money has been taken out.

CCTV

Many towns and cities have closed circuit television (CCTV) cameras which record people as they go about their daily lives. In shops, trains, stations and offices, closed circuit television cameras film people moving around. Cameras on the motorway record the cars travelling, where they are going and what speed they are doing. The number plate can be recognised by automatic number recognition (ANR) camera systems, so you can identify the owner of the car. Face recognition systems are also being introduced.

Sam's journey

WHEELS–R–US

CAR RENTAL

VEHICLE DETAILS

CUSTOMER DETAILS

CUSTOMER NAME   MS SAM BROWN
ADDRESS   42 HOVE STREET
          BRIGHTON
LICENCE NO. BROWN12345ABSS
DATE   15.03.10

REG NUMBER   LJIC
MODEL   ALM1
BRANCH FROM BRI
BRANCH TO   PET
METHOD OF PAYMENT
CARD NUMBER 487
SIGNED   Sam

	DATE	TIME		CHARGES
OUT	15.03.2010	09.32	VAT	
IN	16.03.2010	13.00	TOTAL	

COUNTY BANK
BRIGHTON
TRANSACTION RECORD
WITHDRAWAL
DATE: 15MAR2010
TIME: 08.30
AMOUNT: £100.00
REF: GN71509
THANK YOU

SECURITY CAMERA 6783   09:00

Activity

Look at the trail left by Sam, who went on a journey across the country. Can you work out where she was and when? Use a chart like the one below to help you. The first entry has been done for you.

Sam's journey, 15 March 2010

Time	Place	Evidence
8.30a.m.	Brighton	Bank withdrawal slip

Email and internet

Computers keep a record of internet sites you have visited. It is possible to detect these even if the pages on the internet site are deleted or you clear the history of websites visited. Emails are often intercepted for security checks, and intelligence services know who receives and sends the messages.

Information held by organisations

All the government departments have information on us, including the Inland Revenue (tax collection), the vehicle and driving licence offices, the police, the benefits office and the local authority. Increasingly, information from Facebook, Bebo, MySpace and so on, is being used by the police, insurance companies and employers. People who use loyalty cards in supermarkets are sometimes surprised to find out that their shopping habits are tracked so that they can be targeted with adverts for particular goods.

M23 JUNCTION 10 15.03.10 10:03 70MPH

THE AVENUE
LADIES FASHIONS
CAMBRIDGE HIGH ST.
VAT NO. 1234567890

DATE: 15.03.10   TIME: 14.00

DRESS   £30.00

SWITCH SALE: 4567 8996 7654 3210

TOTAL   £30.00

PHOENIX SERVICE STATION
PHOENIX SERVICES
M23
CRAWLEY
VAT NO. 1234567890

DATE: 15.03.10   TIME: 10:15

SWITCH NO. 4567 8996 7654 3210

20 LITRES PETROL

£25.00

TOTAL

CAMBRIDGE STATION CCTV   18:30   15.03.10

CAMBRIDGE CENTRE CCTV   19:00   15.03.10

MY-MOBILE
THE MOBILE PHONE COMPANY

MS SAM BROWN
42 HOVE ROAD
BRIGHTON

MOBILE PHONE NUMBER
07291 654321

STATEMENT

LOCATION	DATE	TIME	DURATION	NUMBER	AMOUNT
CAMBRIDGE	15.03.10	13.50	4.02	07304 123456	£0.52

CAMBRIDGE HOTEL

NO. OF GUESTS   2

TIME: 22.30   DATE: 15.03.10
MAIN MEAL   £15.00
MAIN MEAL   £15.00
WINE   £12.50

£42.50

VISA DEBIT: 4876 5432 2123 4578

A right to privacy?

Activity

Work in a small group and look at the situations below.

1 Think about whether Sam should be found, or her movements tracked in each of them. Give your reasons in each case.
2 Choose one of the cases where you think Sam should not be found or her movements tracked. Say why you think her right to privacy should be protected in this case.
3 When can surveillance be helpful?
4 When could individuals or governments put it to unpleasant or dangerous uses?

A Sam has forgotten to take some essential medicine with her on the trip and her son is frantically worried that she will become ill.

B Sam is suspected of belonging to a terrorist organisation that may be planning to explode a bomb in Cambridge.

C Sam's boss suspects she is sending in fiddled expense claims and wants to know how far she really did travel.

D Sam is very critical of the government and belongs to a group of activists who are planning a peaceful demonstration at a conference in the north of the country.

E Sam's mother has been involved in a serious accident and has been rushed to hospital in Brighton.

F A robbery took place at a shop in Cambridge at about 1.45p.m. Sam's car shows up on a CCTV camera in the area near the time of the robbery. All suspects are being checked by the police.

G Sam's husband suspects she is having an affair with a man in Cambridge and is having her movements tracked by a private detective.

H Sam is a spy and is passing on secrets to an agent from another country.

DISCUSS

Do you think that we live in a 'surveillance society'? Do you think surveillance might threaten our civil liberties? Why or why not?

Computers – the spies in our homes

More and more organisations are encouraging us to use the internet when we deal with them. Banks, online shops, the tax office, the vehicle licensing office, electricity and gas providers – the list is endless. From the point of view of the organisation, this makes good sense. It is quicker for people to provide information and make payments.

Sometimes we voluntarily provide very personal information about ourselves on social networking sites like Facebook, Bebo or MySpace.

However, we are also being warned about the dangers of revealing too much information about ourselves, for several reasons:

- The information might be used in different ways from those we intended when we provided it, e.g. when applying for jobs.
- Our personal information can be accessed by hackers, who might use or sell the information for criminal purposes.
- Once our information is out there in 'cyberspace', we have no way of changing or deleting it.

For young people, the greatest risks come from social networking sites. Here is what some young people have said about the dangers.

Activity

1 Working in small groups, come up with five tips for using social networking sites safely.
2 Find out what advice the Information Commissioners Office gives to young people, to help them enjoy networking sites at www.ico.gov.uk/Youth.aspx.
3 Design a poster for your school to warn students of the dangers and advise them how to use these sites safely.

Tim, eighteen, said:

" I've heard of bullies using social networking sites to get at people. One girl in my class had her whole Bebo page copied, and all her photos were edited to say really nasty things about her. You have to be really careful with passwords, because if someone gets into your profile they can change what's written there. They can even send messages to your friends, pretending to be you. "

Alisha, sixteen, said:

" I designed a MySpace profile page for my friends' band. They uploaded their songs, some of which included spiteful lyrics about a boy in my year. The songs were really mean and I asked my friends to take them off the page but they wouldn't. When the boy complained to teachers about the songs, my friends said that I had made the MySpace page. I was called in to see the headmaster and I got told off, even though I hadn't written the songs. "

There have also been cases of social networking sites being used by sexual predators to 'groom' young people for under-age sex.

" The Evening Telegraph *(Derby)* revealed that an eleven-year-old girl had been 'groomed' online for about eight weeks after being targeted in a chatroom. The swift actions of her mum in alerting the police resulted in the offender being caught but not before the girl had sent images of herself to the middle-aged man. "

1.6 Freedom of information

As we have seen, the government and police have a lot of information about the public. So how much can we know about them? Many people think that, in a free country, everyone should have the right to know about how publicly-funded organisations work. This means having the right to know about:

- central and local government
- the health service
- schools, colleges and universities
- the police
- all the many bodies that are funded by the taxpayer (for example, the BBC and the courts).

The Freedom of Information Act was passed by parliament in the UK in 2000 and came into force on 1 January 2005. Any person can make a request for information from publicly-funded organisations under the Act – there are no restrictions on your age, nationality, or where you live, and it is free.

DISCUSS

Why should the public be able to find out about how decisions are made and how money is spent by public bodies?

All you have to do is write to (or email) the public authority that you think holds the information you want.

You should make sure that you include:

- your name
- an address where you can be contacted
- a description of the information that you want.

An example is given below.

> Alex Turner
> 54 High Street
> Billington
> XX6 1NN
>
> Chief Executive
> Billington National Health
> Service Trust
> Station Road
> Billington
> XX12 1YY
>
> Dear Sir/Madam,
>
> My mother has had poor treatment in your hospital, particularly during the night from staff who work for agencies. There appear to be no other staff on duty. Under the Freedom of Information Act I would like to see your policy statement on monitoring agency staff to make sure they treat patients properly.
>
> Yours faithfully,
>
> Alex Turner

An example of the use of the Freedom of Information Act

In 2008, the Freedom of Information Act was used to try to persuade the Houses of Parliament to reveal how much MPs were claiming in expenses. The parliamentary officials refused and MPs tried to exclude themselves from the law on freedom of information. A judge ruled that the information was 'in the public interest' and should be provided. Parliament had to agree. However, in order to protect people's addresses, the information was going to be provided with some details blacked out.

In 2009, a daily newspaper got hold of a disk with all the information on it, and published it over a period of a month. It revealed that some MPs claimed for things they shouldn't and also avoided paying tax on the sale of homes paid for through expenses. This led to a big scandal, and the resignation of the Speaker. A number of MPs stood down or were sacked. Some faced investigation by the police or the tax office.

Grounds for refusal

There are rules about whether you can get information or not. You can be refused information if:

- public access to the information threatened national security or the defence of the country
- the information could put someone's health and safety at risk
- the information gives personal details of an individual
- the search for the information would cost a public body more than £450 (£600 for central government).

You can appeal against a refusal, and you must get an explanation.

Activity

1 Read the cases below and decide, in each case, whether the information would be available or not according to the rules.
2 Do you think this information should be available to everyone?

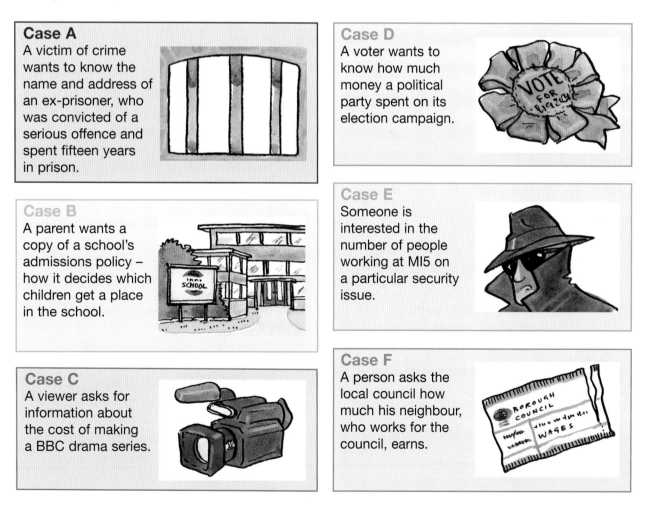

Case A
A victim of crime wants to know the name and address of an ex-prisoner, who was convicted of a serious offence and spent fifteen years in prison.

Case B
A parent wants a copy of a school's admissions policy – how it decides which children get a place in the school.

Case C
A viewer asks for information about the cost of making a BBC drama series.

Case D
A voter wants to know how much money a political party spent on its election campaign.

Case E
Someone is interested in the number of people working at MI5 on a particular security issue.

Case F
A person asks the local council how much his neighbour, who works for the council, earns.

1.7 Equal opportunities for all?

In the UK there are laws that protect people's rights as well as the Human Rights Act. It is against the law to discriminate against someone because of their race or their sex, and there is also some protection from discrimination for people with disabilities. Discrimination can happen in lots of different areas of life: housing, benefits, schools, hospitals, and particularly at work.

Activity

1 The laws shown in the panel on the right make it illegal to discriminate against people directly or indirectly or, in the case of disabled people, to treat them 'less favourably' than non-disabled people.
In which of the following examples of people applying for jobs might the law have been broken?

A A job in a club requires female workers to wear a skirt, but one applicant wears trousers for religious reasons and therefore does not get the job.

B A job at a call centre is advertised. Applicants must have 'clear spoken English'.

C A single mother wants a live-in nanny, and advertises for a 'young woman'.

D An applicant does not get a job because she would not be able to do shift work as she has children.

E Someone does not get an office job because he is a wheelchair user. There are stairs at the offices and no lift.

F A worker does not get a job on a building site because it involves wearing a safety helmet and, as a Sikh, he wears a turban.

Discrimination and the law

The **Sex Discrimination Act 1975** makes it illegal to discriminate against someone because of their sex. The **Equal Pay Act 1970** gives an individual the right to the same pay and benefits as a person of the opposite sex in the same employment, where the man and the woman are doing similar work or work of equal value.

The **Race Relations Act 1976** (amended 2000) makes it illegal to discriminate against someone because of colour, race, nationality or ethnic origin.

Both direct and indirect discrimination under these Acts are against the law.

- Direct discrimination is when someone is treated badly simply because of their sex, colour, race, nationality or ethnic origin – for example, if a company refuses to give a woman a job because she has children, but does employ men with children.
- Indirect discrimination is when certain conditions are unfair for some people – for example, if a job involves wearing clothes that cannot be worn by people of a particular religion.

The **Disability Discrimination Act 2005** gives disabled people rights in the areas of employment, education, access to goods, facilities and services including private clubs and transport services. It also makes it easier for disabled people to rent property and for tenants to make disability-related adaptations. The Act requires public bodies to promote equality of opportunity for disabled people. It also allows the Government to set minimum standards so that disabled people can use public transport easily.

Prejudice and discrimination

The equal opportunities laws were brought in to stop people treating others unfairly by discriminating against them. Discrimination means stopping someone from getting a job, a home or some other benefit, because of prejudices.

When people make a judgement about someone without knowing that person, it is called 'prejudice'. In other words, they prejudge a person because of their age, sex, race, disability, social class, accent, size, sexuality … whatever. Most people have prejudiced attitudes – some negative, some positive. For example, we may think that all grey-haired old ladies are law-abiding.

Activity

2 Look at the cartoons below and decide what prejudice is being shown.

23

Activity

1 There are two jobs available in Barringtons, a large building firm: a qualified plumber and an office manager. There are three applicants for each job, and your task is to decide who to appoint. Work in pairs and read the job descriptions carefully. Then look at the qualifications and experience of each candidate on pages 24–5. Decide who should get each job and be prepared to give reasons for your choice.

PLUMBER
Job description

A qualified plumber is required to work on a Barringtons housing development out of town. The work will involve installing water supplies, sanitation, central heating and waste disposal systems. You will be expected to work well in a team, and you will need to be familiar with building regulations. The job will be full-time for 40 hours per week, with occasional overtime, and some weekend work.

Office Manager
Job description

An office manager is required at Barringtons' headquarters in the city centre. The work will involve organising and supervising the work of the office so that it runs smoothly and efficiently. You will arrange meetings, allocate work to administrative staff, order equipment and stock, control the office budget and be responsible for health and safety in the office. The job will be full-time for 37 hours per week.

Applicant 1: Plumber

Wendy Asaria, 25 years old, has an NVQ level 3 Plumbing qualification obtained five years ago at college on day release from an apprenticeship.
She spent two years working with her father and then three years in a large building firm. She wants a job nearer to home because she has twin boys at school in the area.

Applicant 2: Plumber

Thomas Bennett, 43 years old, has a certificate from City & Guilds in basic plumbing gained 10 years ago. Since then, he has worked on small domestic jobs on his own as a self-employed plumber.
He now wants a more secure job in a company, where he can make pension contributions.

Applicant 3: Plumber

Amrit Kapoor, 59 years old, has worked as a plumber all his life, at first in India, where he gained qualifications equivalent to NVQ level 4. For the last fifteen years in Britain he has worked in the family firm owned by his uncle. The firm has recently closed because of the economic difficulties.

Applicant 1: Office Manager

Jane Johnson, 55 years old, is an ex-teacher who used to run a large English department in a comprehensive school. She has had some ill health, and is now wheelchair-bound with severe arthritis in her knees. She has a degree in English and a post-graduate teaching qualification.

Applicant 2: Office Manager

Bertie Mackintosh, 42 years old, has had office administration jobs for eight years. He trained originally as a librarian and has a level 3 award in Library and Information Services. He was a senior librarian before leaving to take up a post as an office manager in the Post Office. He is looking for a job nearer to home, so that he can look after his children, since his divorce.

Applicant 3: Office Manager

Richard Bauer, 61 years old, has retired from his post as health and safety inspector at the local council. He does not qualify for his old-age pension until 65 and wants to continue working. He led the team of health and safety officers at the council for twenty years, and has run training courses on health and safety.

Activity

2 When you and your partner have decided who gets which job, announce your decisions to the whole class. Did everyone agree?

a) What sorts of things affected your decisions?

b) Were there any times when your decisions were affected by a person's age, sex, race, disability or family?

c) In the real world, do you think these things ever affect decisions about who gets a job? Explain your answer.

1.8 Access for all?

Many disabled people feel that they are still denied the right to participate fully in society, despite the Disability Discrimination Act 2005, because their access to public places and workplaces is restricted. This may prevent them getting to the places as well as getting into them.

Activity

Look at the illustration on pages 26–7.

1 Identify all the things that might make moving around and getting into places difficult for people with disabilities. As well as wheelchair users, consider people who use walking aids and those who are deaf, blind, or have other impairments.
2 Identify the things that have been done to improve access.
3 What do you think still needs to be done to make sure public places and workplaces are accessible for disabled people?
4 How accessible is your school?

Attitudes towards disability

Changing attitudes towards disabled people can be just as important as removing physical barriers to access.

Activity

1 Read the statements below.
   a) What do they show you about attitudes towards people with disabilities?
   b) What do you think are the main ways in which this situation can be improved in shops, transport and public places?
   c) Choose one of the statements and write a letter of complaint to the organisation involved.

A This clothes store opened recently and I wanted to look around. Unfortunately, disabled people's needs have not been considered by the people who designed the layout of the store. It is impossible to go between the rails in a wheelchair or to reach anything. I find clothes get caught on the handles of my chair. The cash desk is too high to reach in comfort and the changing rooms are impossible to get into.

D I find that some beauticians on make-up counters cannot understand why I, as a disabled person, would want to buy and wear make-up. They are usually pretty patronising. It is very rare to find someone who will take time with me and help me choose the best products. Recently a young woman was quite short with me when I asked for a demonstration of some products, so I bought nothing.

B I was booked on to a low cost flight for my holiday to Majorca. Unfortunately, there were other wheelchair users booked on to the same flight and the airline said it could not take more than three of us for 'safety reasons'. We had a long argument about it, before they agreed to take us all. It was humiliating.

C I work in central London and the quickest way for me to get to work would be by underground train. However, there are no step-free entrances or exits at any of the tube stations nearest to my place of work, so I have to travel on the slow route via bus. It means leaving the house 45 minutes earlier.

E I am visually impaired, but would love to meet a girlfriend. Normal dating agencies have refused to allow me to sign up so I have had to join a specialist dating agency for disabled people. Does this mean that people with disabilities are not expected to date able-bodied people?

There is some evidence that attitudes are slowly changing. For example, there was great interest in athletes who won medals in the Beijing Paralympics (2008).

A double gold medallist, an MBE, 2008 BBC Young Sports Personality of the Year at only fourteen?

Absolutely amazing!

Ellie, from Walsall, West Midlands, but who now lives and trains in Swansea, has achondroplasia or dwarfism. She has been swimming since the age of five but was inspired to train as an elite athlete after watching a British victory at the Athens Paralympics in 2004.

She tells it best in her own words: 'I was watching my hero, Nyree Lewis, winning the gold medal in the 100 metres backstroke and I just told myself that I would like to do that.'

So the family upped and moved to Swansea where there's a high-performance swimming centre, and the rest is history. And despite being feted as a hero and held up as an example to youngsters everywhere (which she undoubtedly is) she remains as down to earth and humble as you can imagine.

'Although there's so much going on in my life these days I don't get distracted from my schoolwork,' she says. 'I use the same concentration in school as I do with the swimming.'

And as well as getting on with her studies, Ellie still trains twice a day at 6a.m. and again at 5p.m., six days a week. And she says her friends treat her exactly as they did before – although she did get to 'switch on the Christmas lights in Walsall'.

To the able bodied it seems as though Ellie has overcome so much, but she doesn't see it that way and rarely mentions her disability. When asked about it she once replied: 'I don't know when I became aware that I was smaller than other people. As far as I'm concerned I'm the same as everyone else. But I hope I can show disabled people what they can do. I want people who are disabled and not disabled who like swimming to see what they can achieve with it.'

Ellie was appointed a Member of the Order of the British Empire (MBE) in 2009. At fourteen she is the youngest person to have ever received this honour.

And what does she make of all this? 'While feeling as though I am living in a fairy tale, I want to work hard to keep my feet on the ground,' she says. 'I want to refocus my efforts on my training and my schoolwork so that by 2012 I can hopefully repay in part the wonderful accolades and affection that I have received.'

Eleanor Simmonds

Activity

Research

2 Find out about other paralympic athletes and medal winners.
  Find out:
  a) what sport(s) they play
  b) what their disability is
  c) the history of their involvement in the sport
  d) about their training and preparation programme.

3 You are a radio interviewer. Draw up a list of questions you would like to ask one of the people you have researched.

4 Put together a five-minute radio broadcast on the issues facing disabled athletes and what able-bodied people can learn from them.

5 If possible, invite a disabled person to come into school to talk about their life and their ideas.

Reflection

How well do you think you're doing?
Think back over the work you have done in Section 1.

Skills

- Draw a chart like the one below, and give yourself a grade from 1 to 5, where 1 is the lowest and 5 is the highest.
- Give evidence for your score and say how you could improve your skills.

How well can you ... ?	1	2	3	4	5	Evidence for your score?	How can you improve?
explain your opinions							
justify your opinions							
give evidence for your opinions							
make decisions about balancing rights							
negotiate between different points of view							

Understanding

- Answer TRUE or FALSE to the following statements:

  1 Owning property is a human right.
  2 Racial discrimination is against the law.
  3 The police have the right to arrest anyone they like.
  4 All transport should, by law, be accessible to disabled people.
  5 Newspapers can publish anything they want.

- Give two factors that might influence a person's opinions on abortion.
- Complete this sentence:
  'In a free society, people will always disagree about their rights. An example of this is ...'
- Talk to another pupil and discuss what you think was the most important thing you learned in this section.

Section 2

National government and national politics

The UK is a democracy. This means that the national government is chosen by the people of the country in a general election. If the people are not happy with the government it can be voted out at the next election. All democracies have laws to protect the rights of people in those countries, such as freedom of speech and the right to a fair trial. In the UK the job of parliament is to make laws, discuss important issues and keep an eye on the government, to make sure it is running the country properly. But it is also important for people to know how our democracy works and take part in it. In the past, a lot of people fought hard for the right of all adults to vote and to have a say in the way the country is run.

KEY WORDS

campaign

constituency

democracy

election

manifesto

parliament

political party

pressure group

Assessing your progress
In this section you will be assessing how well you can:

* discuss different ideas, opinions and beliefs
* take account of other people's views
* make a case and argue for a particular point of view, and challenge the arguments of others
* plan responsible action to get your views across and influence people
* understand how the UK is governed and how parliament works.

We all like to think that we live in a free country – a democracy where people can influence the Government and have the right to say and do what they like. But in real life we can't say and do what we like: we have to obey laws and control our behaviour because what we do affects other people. These laws also protect us from other people. So, in a democracy we have to balance our freedom against protection and control. We have to be very watchful because we can easily lose some of our freedom if we are not careful. So, where do you stand on what is important in our democracy?

Definition of democracy

> **"** Government of the people, by the people, for the people. **"**

Activity

Read the statements on pages 32–3 and decide whether you agree with them, do not agree or are not so sure about them. Give reasons for your answers and explain how you would change a statement you don't agree with so you would be able to agree with it. You could draw up a table and put the statements into one of four columns:

Agree	Disagree	Not so sure about	Would change to ...

I would prefer to live in a country where ...

A ... there are regular elections to choose the people who are going to govern the country.

B ... the TV and newspapers are censored by the Government.

C ... only men are allowed to vote.

D ... people can follow any religion they like.

E ... newspapers and magazines can print any stories they like about people's private lives.

F ... the police do exactly what the Government tells them.

G ... everyone can get together to discuss their views or hold meetings.

H ... people are allowed to protest and demonstrate if they don't like what the Government is doing.

I ... people have complete freedom of speech.

J ... there is a system of identity cards with lots of information about us to protect us from terrorism.

K ... for serious crimes, everybody has the right to a trial by a jury of their fellow citizens.

L ... everyone obeys the laws including members of the Government.

M ... if people are arrested they have to be told what they are charged with and there must be a trial.

N ... people should have the right to see any records or documents that the Government or local councils or schools and hospitals have on them.

O ... the police should have all the powers they need to protect us from terrorism, such as entering houses, listening in on telephone calls, holding people for questioning.

P ... the Government directly controls judges and the courts of law.

Q ... people should not be allowed to say things that are racist or offend another person's religion.

R ... the Government should be allowed to keep what it does secret.

S ... the people's representatives can question the Government to check what it is doing and make sure it is not corrupt and is acting properly.

Three basic principles of democracy

There is disagreement about what the word 'democracy' means and democracies around the world are different. But most people agree that these three principles are important ones:

1 Freedom of speech, belief and association for everyone.
2 The rule of law and that everyone is equal under the law.
3 The government represents the people of that country and is accountable to the people of that country.

DISCUSS

1 Which of the statements on pages 32–3 match or are connected to one of the basic principles of democracy?
2 Discuss in class any different opinions about the statements and which ones are particularly important in a democracy.
3 Why do you think it is important that 'ordinary' people get involved in politics?

33

2.2 Political parties

One way of getting your views heard in a democracy is by joining or supporting a political party. A political party is an organised group of people with a leader and members. It has a set of views that the members agree with. Parties put up candidates at elections so that these people can be voted into positions of power, nationally or locally. People join a political party because they agree with what it stands for. They also want to help the party win elections and put their ideas into practice.

Activity

You are going to create your own political party.

1 Work in groups of four or five. Imagine that you want to make this country a better place in which to live. What would you change? In your group, choose three things that you would like to change. You can get some ideas from this page, or you can come up with some of your own.

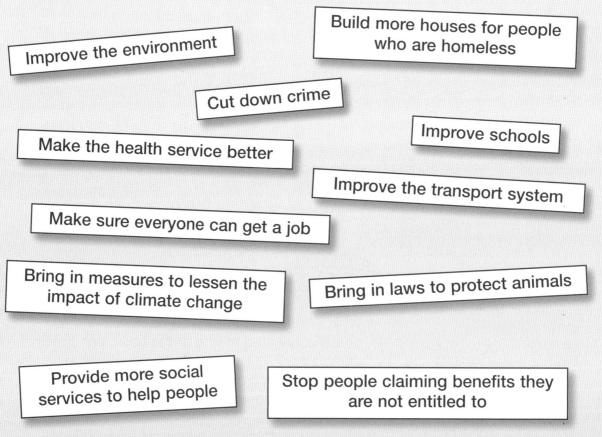

Help poorer people in the rest of the world

Improve the environment

Build more houses for people who are homeless

Cut down crime

Improve schools

Make the health service better

Improve the transport system

Make sure everyone can get a job

Bring in measures to lessen the impact of climate change

Bring in laws to protect animals

Provide more social services to help people

Stop people claiming benefits they are not entitled to

2 Give your party a name and elect a leader.

Our party is suggesting a number of ways to improve the environment in which we all live.

3 Draw a chart like the one on the right, and fill it in. (The completed row is just an example to help you.)

   a) In the first column put the three issues you have chosen.

   b) Decide what you want to do about these issues. These are your **aims**. Put these in the second column.

   c) Decide how you are going to do it. These are your **policies**. Put these in the third column.

Name of our party:		
Our three issues	What we want to do (our aims)	How we can achieve this (our policies)
Climate change	Reduce the amount of carbon monoxide produced. Save energy and cut down on use of petrol. Find alternative ways of producing energy.	Stop using coal-fuelled power stations. Cut down use of big cars by taxing them more. Encourage people to insulate their houses by giving them grants. Build more wind farms.

4 When you have agreed your policies, you have to convince other people that you are right. You have to plan your **campaign**.

   a) Use the chart to write your **party manifesto**. This sets out the main things your party wants to do (aims) and how you are going to achieve them (policies).

   b) Discuss how you can persuade other people to agree with your views.

   c) Design campaign posters and put them up in the classroom.

   d) Write a three-minute speech for the leader of the party to give to the whole class. Invite some visitors to listen to the speeches. Your visitors can vote on which party was the most persuasive.

Note: You can follow up this activity by running the mock election on page 42.

Political parties in the UK

We hear about the main political parties all the time because they are in the news: the Labour Party, the Conservative Party, the Liberal Democrats. There are, however, many political parties that we hear less about. The following political parties all have Members of Parliament:

Conservatives
Conservative Party

LIBERAL DEMOCRATS
Liberal Democrats

Labour
Labour Party

Plaid PLAID CYMRU
Plaid Cymru

SF Sinn Fein

UUP
Ulster Unionist Party

Scottish National Party

DUP
Democratic Unionist Party

RESPECT THE RESPECT PARTY
Respect Coalition

SDLP Social Democratic and Labour Party
Social Democratic and Labour Party

Other political parties have no Members of Parliament at the moment. Some of them are quite small. The Electoral Commission's Register of Political Parties lists over 120 organisations! Look at the logos of just a few:

Green Party FAIR IS WORTH FIGHTING FOR
Green Party of England and Wales

UKIP
UK Independence Party

animals count
Animals Count

LIBERTARIAN for life, liberty and prosperity
Libertarian Party

MONSTER RAVING LOONY
Monster Raving Loony Party

NLP National Liberal Party
National Liberal Party

Activity

Split the class up into small groups. Use the internet to find out about these political parties.

1 Some groups can find information about the main parties:
   - Who is the leader?
   - What are the names of other key people and what jobs do they do?
   - What are the main aims of the party?
   - What is in their party manifesto or what are the main things they want to see done?

Other groups can find out similar or any particularly interesting information about one of the smaller parties. Some of the smaller parties present themselves in a very different way to the main parties or have very specific objectives.

2 When you have finished, each group should make a brief presentation about the party they have researched.

General elections

Political parties present their policies to the people of Britain in general elections. This is when the voters or 'electorate' choose the Members of Parliament (MPs) who are to represent them in Parliament in the House of Commons. Each MP represents the people who live in a particular area of the country called a constituency. You do not have to belong to a party to become an MP. You can be an 'Independent'.

The political party that wins the majority of seats (has most MPs) in the House of Commons forms the government and runs the country. The leader of this party becomes the Prime Minister. The party with the second largest number of MPs forms the Official Opposition.

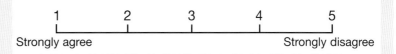

Why vote?

Some people don't bother to vote in general elections. In some countries, like Australia, it is compulsory to vote.

1 Look at the arguments below. For each one, rank them on a scale of 1–5 by how much you agree with them.

1	2	3	4	5
Strongly agree				Strongly disagree

2 Compare your rankings in class and discuss whether you think it is important to vote or not.

Do you think people should be made to vote and fined if they don't?

A People in the past have fought for the right to vote and we should take our responsibility seriously. In some countries, people are not allowed to vote and have no way of changing or influencing their governments.

B All the main parties are the same. It does not make any difference who wins the election.

C If you don't vote you can't complain about the Government when it does things you don't like.

D MPs in Parliament make laws and decisions that affect our lives in a big way. We should take part in electing these MPs.

E Once MPs get elected, they don't listen to us and do what they want. So there is no point in voting.

F MPs are only out for their own personal gain, for money or for power and influence, so I won't vote for them.

G I don't understand what they are going on about and I am not that interested, so I won't bother to vote.

Do we need a new voting system?

First past the post (FPTP)

The system used in the UK for parliamentary elections is called the first past the post system. This means that the person who wins the most votes in a constituency is elected as the MP and takes their seat in Parliament. The runners-up get nothing.

Activity

1 Look at the example on the right.
  a) Who won?
  b) What percentage of people voted for this person?
  c) What percentage did not vote for this person?

Proportional Representation (PR)

Some people think that the FPTP system is unfair because the votes of lots of people don't count. They would prefer a system called proportional representation (PR). Under this the seats in Parliament would be shared out by all the parties according to the total vote they received in the election.

Example

Suppose a total of 1000 people voted. You can see the number of votes each candidate received and their percentage of the vote:

SMITH   400 votes   (40%)
AHMED   300 votes   (30%)
JONES   150 votes   (15%)
CAMPBELL   100 votes   (10%)
GREEN   50 votes   (5%)

Research

2 There are a number of voting systems based on PR including the list system, single transferable vote and the alternative vote. Find out about one of these systems and where it is used.

Example
Here is a simple example to show the difference between the FPTP system and PR.

Party	Eastside constituency	Westside constituency	Northside constituency	Southside constituency	Central constituency	Share of total vote
Union Party	500	400	400	200	500	2000 (40%)
People's Party	300	390	610	400	300	2000 (40%)
Planet Party	200	210	190	200	200	1000 (20%)
The winning party is ...						

In real life, quite complicated systems are used so that the percentage of seats a party wins is about the same as the percentage of votes they get.

Activity

3 In the chart on page 38 there are five separate constituencies in the five columns. If you read down each column you can work out which party won the election. This is the 'First Past The Post' system.

a) How many seats did the Union Party and People's Party win?

b) How many did the Planet Party win?

4 Suppose these five constituencies were put together in a region and the five seats were given out according to the share of the vote they got (look in the final column). You get a seat per 1000 votes. This is a 'Proportional Representation' system.

a) How many seats would the parties get now?

b) What is the difference between the two systems?

FPTP is the best system because ...	PR is the best system because ...
• It is simple to understand – the person who wins the most votes is elected. • One MP represents the people in a particular constituency. People know who they are voting for and who to go to represent their views. • It usually creates a clear winner with one party with the majority of MPs. This means that the Government can make clear decisions and get its laws through the House of Commons. This creates strong government. • PR often leads to lots of parties being elected and this can lead to a hung parliament or coalition government where nobody is clearly in charge. This creates weak governments. • PR gives more power to smaller parties than they deserve as bigger parties need their support to win votes in Parliament. It can allow extremist parties to get seats.	• Everybody's vote counts. People don't feel that their votes are wasted, so more people are encouraged to vote in elections. • It is fairer because parties win seats according to the percentage of the votes they get in the whole election. • It helps smaller parties gain seats in Parliament and voters get a wider choice of parties which are more likely to represent their views. • It often leads to coalition governments which are good because they stop one party from becoming too powerful. It means parties have to agree on policies and laws, so you get ones more people agree with. • In the FPTP system a party can win an election when, overall, more people have voted against it than voted for it.

Activity

5 Work in pairs.

a) Choose the two arguments that you most agree with in the table above.

b) Which do you think is the fairest system?

c) Which system do you think produces the best government?

d) Write a short essay agreeing or disagreeing with this statement:

'It is time the UK adopted a proportional representation PR voting system. This would be fairer and produce better governments.'

In your essay, use the arguments in the table above and say why you agree with some arguments and disagree with others.

All citizens of the United Kingdom over the age of eighteen are eligible for election to Parliament, unless they are, or have been, in prison, have certain kinds of mental illness or are members of the House of Lords. You could be an MP when you are eighteen.

Activity

These pictures show the stages in becoming an MP but they are in the wrong order. Put them in the correct order. If there are any words you don't understand, you will find them explained in the glossary on pages 93–4.

A Anna Cassidy joins a political party. She works for the party for several years; attending meetings, helping out at election time, raising funds for the party.

B After the vote has ended, the **ballot box** is taken to a hall with all the other ballot boxes in the constituency. The votes are counted. The **Returning Officer** then announces that Anna is the candidate with the most votes. She is now the MP for her constituency and will go to the House of Commons.

E After a number of years Anna decides that she wants to be an MP. She puts her name forward for an interview with the constituency selection committee. Several other people are also interviewed. She is chosen to be her party's candidate at the next election.

D The day of the election arrives. The voters go to a **polling station**. They are each given a **ballot paper** with the names of the candidates on it. They take their paper to a polling booth where no one can see what they are writing. They put an 'X' next to the candidate they want to vote for. Then they put their ballot paper in a sealed metal box.

VOTE HERE

Would it be better to have more 'Independents' in Parliament?

Most MPs are members of political parties but some are 'Independents' who do not belong to a party. Look at the points below and see whether you think it would be better to have more independents.

C Anna has an agent to run her campaign; he organises posters, leaflets and public meetings. Party volunteers canvass for her; this means they go round houses in the constituency explaining what Anna and her party stand for and the policies in the party manifesto.

In the House of Commons the parties have 'whips' – MPs whose job it is to get the other MPs in their party voting the way the leaders of the party want them to vote. This can mean that MPs do more or less as they are told by their party, so things are not properly discussed. Independent MPs do not have to obey party 'whips'.

A different view of whips is that they make sure parties have a clear policy on important issues. This can be useful in that the Government (the party with the largest number of MPs) can get its laws passed and govern strongly.

Independents can play a useful role in Parliament. Because they don't belong to a party they can vote freely for the good of the country and their constituents (the people who elected them). They can vote for what they really believe in.

MPs might do as they are told so that they get more powerful positions in their party or jobs in government if their party comes to power. This might mean that they are more concerned in voting for their own interests than the good of the people who elected them.

You need parties so that there are clear policies about running the country. Independents tend to campaign on a single issue, for example, to stop a hospital being closed or anti-corruption in Parliament, so if you had lots of Independents they might not have clear ideas on a wide range of issues.

F The Prime Minister decides that it is time to call a general election. The Queen dissolves Parliament and the election campaign starts.

DISCUSS

Would you like to see more 'Independent' MPs in the House of Commons?

Run a mock election

Who would like to be voted an MP in your class election? Divide the class into two: one half will be candidates and helpers, the other half will be voters. Candidates and helpers should follow the instructions in the yellow panel. Voters should follow the instructions in the blue panel.

Candidates and helpers

- Five or six members of this group will be the candidates. Each candidate should have one or two helpers.

- The candidates will need to meet to decide which parties they will each represent. Three candidates should represent the main parties, others the smaller parties or made-up parties with their own **manifesto**.

- Candidates and helpers should work out their manifesto together. Each manifesto must state what the party will do about:
  - education
  - transport and roads
  - health.

  Ideas for other policies can also be added. You can use ideas from the activity on pages 34–5.

- Each candidate, with one helper, should visit the groups of voters, tell them about their manifesto plans and listen to what they have to say. You might change your manifesto as a result of this. Meanwhile other helpers can design a poster.

- Candidates should give short two- or three-minute talks to the whole class outlining their manifesto and policy ideas.

Voters

- The voters should form groups of three. These groups should then decide what they want the candidates to do about the following issues:
  - education, e.g. provide more teachers, reduce class sizes
  - transport and roads, e.g. get rid of traffic congestion
  - health, e.g. provide more doctors and nurses.

  Two more issues should be added to this list. Spend 15–20 minutes on this.

- Elect one member of the whole 'voters' group as the Returning Officer who runs the election. Several other 'voters' can play journalists who are reporting on the campaign. They could do this by interviewing candidates and writing headlines to display (e.g. 'Conservative candidate promises tax cuts').

- Candidates should visit the voters to tell them about their ideas and policies and get some information about what the voters are thinking. This gives the voters a chance to influence the candidates. The journalists can interview voters to find out what they think about the candidates' ideas and policies.

- The Returning Officer with some helpers (voters not engaged in other activities) can design and make ballot papers for everyone in the class to use. A sample ballot paper is shown opposite. This group should also make or find a ballot box to put votes in.

Voting will take place at a pre-agreed time. Everyone has a vote, including the candidates and helpers, and the vote is secret. Each voter should have a ballot paper. Mark a cross against the chosen candidate, fold the paper and post it in the ballot box.

Candidates	**X** Mark a cross against your chosen candidate
BROWN, Sam (Monster Raving Loony Party)	
JONES, Frankie (Conservative Party)	
MACDONALD, Angus (Independent)	
PATEL, Rehanna (Liberal Democrats)	
ROBERTS, Chris (Labour Party)	
SMITH, Alice (Green Party)	

The Returning Officer and helpers should make sure that the count of the votes is fair. Journalists could also keep an eye on things. The count should be carried out in public so that everyone can see it. The Returning Officer announces the result to the class. The results should be read out as shown in the example below:

> I *[name]*, being the Returning Officer for *Class [X]* do hereby declare that the votes cast by *Class [X]* in this election are as follows:
>
> | | |
> | --- | --- |
> | Brown, Sam | 10 votes |
> | Jones, Frankie | 3 votes |
> | MacDonald, Angus | 2 votes |
> | Patel, Rehanna | 6 votes |
> | Roberts, Chris | 2 votes |
> | Smith, Alice | 5 votes |
>
> I therefore declare that Sam Brown is duly elected as Member of Parliament for *Class [X]*.

The winner should then make an acceptance speech.

What does an MP do?

In the House of Commons

Representing people

The main job of an MP is to represent the people in their constituency in the House of Commons. It does not matter if the people voted for the MP or not, the MP has to represent all of them. You can 'lobby' your MP – visit or write to him or her to make your views known. An MP can raise issues in the House of Commons and ask the Government questions.

Making laws

MPs play an important part in making laws in the House of Commons. They look carefully at the laws, debate them and suggest changes to them.

Making speeches and taking part in debates

An MP takes part in debates on important issues like national security. He or she may make speeches on these issues or on new laws.

Working on committees

An MP often plays a role on Select Committees. These are groups of MPs from different political parties who focus on a specific issue like transport or the environment. They research and discuss their issues so that they can report on them to the House of Commons and influence the Government.

Outside the House of Commons

Meeting constituents

An MP holds 'surgeries' in the local constituency, usually once a week. This is when people can bring the MP their problems. These may be to do with politics, national issues, or they may be more local about disputes or problems with the local council. Often the MP can persuade others to find solutions or come to agreements. An MP can play an important part in bringing different communities together to prevent misunderstanding and conflict.

Visits and fact finding

An MP visits places like schools, hospitals and day centres, especially in their own constituency. This can provide useful information about people's concerns and difficulties to take back to Parliament.

Travelling

MPs travel all over the UK, often making speeches on behalf of their political party or helping out in election campaigns. Sometimes they travel abroad to find out about international issues such as poverty, debt or women's rights.

Activity

1 You can see that an MP's job is quite demanding. They need to have a wide range of skills and knowledge to be able to do it. Look carefully at the information opposite and then, in pairs or threes, write a job description for a Member of Parliament. You can use the outline on the right. Try to think of at least four items for each category:

knowledge, skills, experience and personal qualities.

2 Find out:
   a) who your MP is
   b) the name of the constituency in which you live
   c) how and when you could meet your MP.

3 Write a letter or email to your MP. He or she will usually have a website which tells you what they are doing and some of the things they are involved in. Working with a partner, choose an issue you are interested in or passionate about. This could be a local issue, such as safety on the streets or the local hospital, or a national or international issue like climate change or helping people in developing countries. In your letter or email, explain your views and ask for the MP's reaction.

Job description for the Member of Parliament for .... constituency

You should have knowledge of ...
e.g. the local area and people.

The following skills will be very useful ...
e.g. good at speaking in public.

Useful experience would be ...
e.g. running a business or other organisation.

You would possess some of the following personal qualities ...
e.g. honesty, able to work well with people.

---

3 Station Road
Sunnydale
Midshire
SU12 1PL

Jenny Poll MP
House of Commons
London
SW1A 0AA

Dear Ms Poll,

I am sure you have heard that they are planning to close Littledeen Primary School. Everybody in our family and all our neighbours are very angry about this. It should be kept open because ...

The Prime Minister and the other members of the Government run the United Kingdom. But they can't do just what they want. They have to explain and account for their actions in the Houses of Parliament. There are two houses: the House of Commons and the House of Lords.

The House of Commons

The House of Commons is the most powerful house and is where the MPs sit. The Government needs the support of the House of Commons to pass laws. If a majority of MPs in the House regularly vote against the Government, it may have to resign. The job of the Opposition in the Commons is to challenge the Government, raise questions about the way it is running the country and make sure it is not corrupt.

What work does the House of Commons do?

- It makes laws.
- It questions the Government and examines what it is doing.
- It keeps a check on the amount of money that the Government spends.
- It holds debates on issues of national importance.

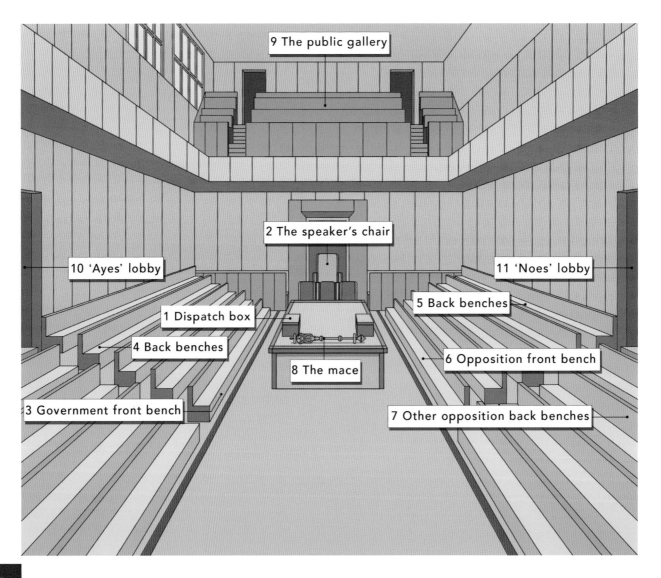

9 The public gallery

2 The speaker's chair

10 'Ayes' lobby

11 'Noes' lobby

1 Dispatch box

5 Back benches

4 Back benches

6 Opposition front bench

8 The mace

3 Government front bench

7 Other opposition back benches

A The Prime Minister stands at the dispatch box to make announcements or answer questions.

B The leaders of the opposition sit on the front bench on the other side from the Government.

C This is the symbol to show the House of Commons is sitting.

D The Speaker is the person who runs debates, calls people to speak and keeps order in the House of Commons.

E Government ministers and the Prime Minister sit on the front bench just behind the dispatch box.

F The MPs from the political party which forms the Government sit on the back benches behind the Government.

G MPs go here when voting in favour of something.

H The MPs who belong to the party of the Opposition sit on the opposite side of the House of Commons facing the Government.

I This is where MPs who belong to the other opposition parties sit.

J MPs go here when they are voting against something.

K This is where members of the public can sit to watch the proceedings in Parliament.

The House of Lords

The House of Lords is not elected. Its members are called 'peers'. Some are, for historical reasons, 'hereditary' peers. Most are 'life' peers which means they are appointed for their lifetime. The main jobs of the House of Lords are to:

- act as a check on the House of Commons to make sure that new laws are discussed thoroughly and not rushed through
- look critically at the work of the Government
- hold debates on important issues which may influence the Government and the House of Commons.

Activity

1 Look at the outline drawing of the inside of the House of Commons opposite. To learn about it, match the numbers 1–11 with one of the letters A–K above.
2 Find out more about the Houses of Parliament and see it in action by going to www.parliament.uk/ education/index.htm.

How would you modernise Parliament?

In recent years there have been calls for Parliament to become more modern, partly because of the way MPs have behaved. It has been called a 'gentleman's club' where the customs and practices are old fashioned and outdated. Many people want Parliament to be more accessible to the people. Reform of Parliament is taking place. How far has it changed and how far should it go?

Activity

Look at the ideas on this page and the next. Firstly, discuss them in small groups and decide what you think. Then, as a whole class, take each one in turn and vote on whether you approve of the change or not. Give your reasons for supporting changes or keeping things as they are.

1 Prime Minister directly elected by the people?

This way people would vote directly for the Prime Minister to be their leader. This person would then form the Government. This Government could be made up of MPs but the Prime Minister would also be able to ask other people to join the Government.

Prime Minister directly elected? Yes/No

LATEST NEWS

FIRST IN BRITISH HISTORY: YOUR CHANCE TO CHOOSE THE PERSON YOU WANT TO BE PRIME MINISTER

VOTE FOR PM

2 Fixed term parliaments?

The maximum life of a Parliament is five years. The Prime Minister can call an election at any time during those five years. Some reformers are calling for a fixed term parliament of four years, so that the Prime Minister has no say in when it is called.

Fixed term parliaments? Yes/No

THE DAILY NEWS

Parliaments to last for a fixed term of four years

3 More power to the House of Commons?

Reformers say the Prime Minister and government has become too strong, so the House of Commons should be given more power to hold the Government in check. This way the Government would have to listen to the people more.

More power to House of Commons? Yes/No

5 MPs more tightly controlled?

MPs would have a clear set of rules and could be sacked if they broke them (e.g. by cheating on their expenses). Or they could be made to spend a certain amount of time talking to people in their constituencies.

MPs more tightly controlled? Yes/No

4 More free votes in the House of Commons?

MPs would be given more freedom to vote with their conscience on any issue or new law. They would not have to do as their parties told them as much.

More free votes? Yes/No

6 More involvement for ordinary people in making laws?

When new laws are being made, members of the public who had special knowledge of a particular area (e.g. stem cell research) could be brought in to help draft the laws. The views of a range of people could be sought on new laws before they become law.

Involve the public more? Yes/No

7 Fewer MPs in the House of Commons?

There would be fewer MPs in the House of Commons. This would make it cheaper to run.

Fewer MPs? Yes/No

8 Full-time job?

Being an MP would be a full-time job. MPs would not be allowed to earn any extra money or have a second job.

Full-time job? Yes/No

9 Monarch no longer head of state?

The monarch has quite a lot of influence in the present system (e.g. they invite the leader of the winning party in an election to form a government, they open parliament, they give the royal assent to Bills before they become laws, see pages 62–3). This would be changed so that Parliament was run and controlled only by people who are elected and the monarch would not play any part in it.

Monarch no longer head of state? Yes/No

10 Elected House of Lords?

The House of Lords would be elected by the people. For instance, the people in it might represent the different regions of the country. There would be no more hereditary lords who get their position by birth or people given lordships by those in power.

Totally elected House of Lords? Yes/No

DISCUSS

Here are some other things that might be changed. Which of them do you agree with?

1 People could be texted on their phones when legislation is going through Parliament and asked to comment.
2 Every MP would have a website that showed what he/she was doing and when they were available to the public.
3 Old customs and old-fashioned clothes around Parliament would be done away with.
4 Modern language and plain English would be used when talking about laws, not outdated language that people do not understand.

How does Parliament make laws?

One of the main jobs of the House of Commons is to pass new laws, change ones that already exist and get rid of ones that no longer serve any useful purpose.

Stages in making a law

A proposed law is set out in what is called a 'Bill'.

1 **First reading** – the Bill is published for MPs to read. There is no discussion or vote.

2 **Second reading** of the Bill and debate – a government minister explains the purpose of the Bill and answers questions about it. If a majority of MPs vote for it, it goes on to the next stage.

3 **Committee stage** – a small committee of MPs look at the details of the Bill. It suggests changes or amendments to the Bill and votes on these.

4 **Report stage** – the committee reports to the House on the Bill. MPs can suggest further changes.

5 **Third reading** – this gives the House a chance to look at the whole Bill with amendments. After a debate, MPs vote for it or reject it.

6 **House of Lords** – the Bill goes to the Lords who check it. They may suggest changes which are discussed with the House of Commons but they cannot stop the Bill becoming law.

7 **The Royal Assent** – the Bill must be signed by the king or queen before it becomes law.

8 **Act of Parliament** – the Bill is now a law.

Making a new law

A new Bill proposes that: **All young people in the UK from the ages of 14 to 18 should carry an identity card.** This card will include a photograph, fingerprint, educational, medical and employment history, and any criminal record.

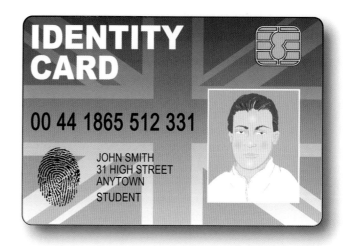

IDENTITY CARD

00 44 1865 512 331

JOHN SMITH
31 HIGH STREET
ANYTOWN

STUDENT

Activity

You are going to debate the Bill in class to help create the new law.

1 a) Half the class will support the Bill and half oppose it. This means that you may have to argue for something that you do not believe. It is important to do this sometimes to see an issue from a different point of view.

b) First, work in groups of three. Use some of the arguments on these pages to develop your own ideas. Choose which one of your group is going to speak in the debate. This means that there should be three or four speakers for each side.

c) Hold the debate.

d) Each group of three can now suggest one amendment (change) to the Bill that they think is fair and good and would improve the Bill. For example, only 18–21 year olds have to carry the card; photograph only, no fingerprints. If a majority of the class votes in favour of an amendment, it is passed.

e) The class now votes on the whole Bill. If the majority vote for it, it becomes law.

Arguments

A It will make life much easier. Instead of producing all sorts of documents, such as your birth certificate, to prove who you are, you just show your identity card. You could use it as ID to show you can buy cigarettes or alcohol or for getting into clubs and bars.

B It will be very expensive to develop and introduce these cards, especially if they have fingerprint or eye recognition. It's not worth it.

C Medical records can be put on the cards. So if you are involved in an accident or are taken seriously ill, medical staff will almost immediately find out your medical history and give you the right treatment.

D It could lead to the police harassing young people, especially those from ethnic minority groups. They are more likely to be asked for their cards. It could hurt relations between the police and young people.

E There would be no problems in sorting out benefits and what the person was entitled to. It would prevent young people coming from other countries claiming benefits to which they are not entitled.

F It does not matter what technology you introduce. People will find a way of producing false identity cards.

G With ID cards, it would be easy to identify trouble makers in clubs, bars or similar places, so these places would become safer. Young people with any record of violence on the card could be excluded.

H It would make Britain like a police state for young people. You would never be able to escape what's on your card. It would be difficult to make a fresh start or achieve anything if you were always weighed down by this complete record of your past.

2.6 Pressure politics

People who have strong opinions on a particular issue often get together to try to influence the people who make decisions, especially government ministers and MPs. They form pressure groups to make sure their views are heard and taken into account. Sometimes they are fighting for their own interests or rights. Sometimes they are fighting for the rights of others or promoting a cause. Often on any particular issues, pressure groups take different positions and oppose each other.

Activity

1 Below are some examples of pressure groups. Which of these, do you think, are fighting for their own interests, and which are fighting for the interests of others or promoting a cause?
2 What other pressure groups have you heard of?
3 Choose one of the groups below, or one of your own choice, to research on the internet. Find out about their aims, methods or campaign tactics and what they have achieved. Present your findings to the rest of the class. Make sure that the class research a range of different pressure groups.

Greenpeace

ASH (Action on Smoking and Health)

Amnesty International

LIBERTY

Liberty

Road Haulage Association

Campaign for Nuclear Disarmament (CND)

Age Concern and Help the Aged

NSPCC

National Society for the Prevention of Cruelty to Children (NSPCC)

The Law Society

Plane Stupid

Countryside Alliance

FATHERSFORJUSTICE

Fathers 4 Justice

What methods do pressure groups use?

Different pressure groups use different methods to influence the government and MPs. Some do it privately by trying to meet powerful people. Some try to get the public on their side because decision makers are more likely to take notice of lots of people.

DISCUSS

Some pressure groups break the law or use violence or intimidation to draw attention to their cause. Do you think this can ever be justified?

Activity

4 Look at the pictures below and describe the different ways pressure groups try to get their message across.

Developing your skills of responsible action

How do you get your views heard and influence people?

We can consider this through the issue of the use of animals in experiments and tests. There are a number of pressure groups which operate in this field which use a range of tactics. You can find out more about them by looking at their websites. Here are some.

The **Animal Liberation Front** consists of small groups of people all over the world that carries out direct action to liberate animals from places where they believe animals are abused, such as laboratories, factory farms and fur farms, and to inflict economic damage to those who profit from the misery and exploitation of animals. You can find out more from their website: www.animalliberationfront.com

People for the Ethical Treatment of Animals (PETA) believes that animals deserve the most basic rights. Animals are not ours to use for food, clothing, entertainment, experimentation, or for any other reason. PETA educates policymakers and the public about cruelty to animals and promotes an understanding of the right of all animals to be treated with respect. You can find out more from their website: www.peta.org.uk

THIS IS ANIMAL EXPERIMENTATION

Don't let anyone tell you different.
PeTA

The ultimate aim of the **Royal Society for the Prevention of Cruelty to Animals (RSPCA)** is the replacement of animal experiments with humane alternatives. Until this can be achieved, they work constructively with all those involved in the regulation, use and care of laboratory animals to promote practical measures that will help reduce the number of animals used, and ensure that animals experience the minimum of suffering and have the best possible quality of life. The RSPCA does not condone the use of violence to support these aims. You can find out more from their website: www.rspca.org.uk

Pro-Test is an Oxford-based group campaigning in favour of continued animal testing as crucially necessary to further medical science. It aims to raise public awareness of the benefits of animal research. It stands for science, reasoned debate and, above all, the promotion of the welfare of mankind. It supports non-violent protest and condemns those using violence or intimidation to further their goals. You can find out more from their website: www.pro-test.org.uk

Activity

1 The Government allows experiments which use animals. You are going to draw up a campaign action-plan to get your views heard on this issue and write an account of how you would go about this.

a) You need to decide what your views are on the topic. There are some arguments below to get you started but you should do more research and collect evidence. You can use the websites listed opposite to get your research going. Write down your position and justify it.

b) Decide what tactics/methods you intend to use to raise public awareness and get people on your side (e.g. poster, website, petition) and explain your choice. How are you going to get your group noticed?

c) Write down which decision makers/ influential people or organisations you would approach (e.g. MP, celebrity, newspapers or TV) and how you would do it.

d) Write down any other action (e.g. direct action) you would take to get your views across.

Against animal testing

- The experiments cause the animals pain and suffering.
- Animals are treated cruelly by being confined in small cages.
- It is wrong to use animals in this way for the benefit of human beings.
- Animals share the earth with us and deserve respect and humane treatment.

For animal testing

- Animal testing saves human lives, e.g. fighting diseases such as cancer.
- There is no real alternative to using animals in tests.
- To stop tests would hold back medical progress.
- Most animals in laboratories in the UK are kept in reasonable conditions and well treated.

Activity

Get your views heard on a local issue

2 You might feel strongly about something going on in your local community such as the closure of a school or a new building development. Plan a campaign to get your views heard.

a) Create your own pressure group of people who share similar views.

b) Research the issue fully so you know a lot about it and can develop a strong argument to support your views.

c) Work out ways to raise awareness and get local people on your side.

d) Target decision makers/influential people in the local area (e.g. councillors, MP, local newspaper/ radio station, or local celebrity).

e) Work out how to approach these people, (e.g. write a letter, email).

f) Develop tactics to get your views heard and to put your message across.

g) Do it!

h) Review your action: what worked and what didn't? What would you change to improve the way you did it?

A country needs a government to:

• protect citizens and keep them safe
• look after their welfare
• watch over the employment of citizens
• look after the environment
• run the economy.

The Government makes decisions about how the country is run and puts these decisions into action, for example, building more schools and hospitals, fighting in wars and creating new jobs.

Activity

How does the Government work in the UK?

1 a) Match each of the descriptions A–I opposite with one of the boxes below.

b) Using the boxes, draw an illustrated chart (or one with notes written on it) to show the UK system of government and its relationship to the Houses of Parliament and the voters. You can add information from other parts of this section.

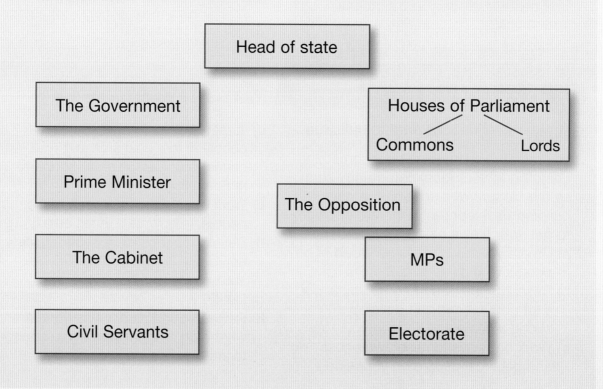

Head of state

The Government

Houses of Parliament

Commons   Lords

Prime Minister

The Opposition

The Cabinet

MPs

Civil Servants

Electorate

G This is made up of the most important ministers who are in charge of the big government departments such as the Home Office, Foreign Office, Department of Health and Department of Work and Pensions. They work with the Prime Minister to decide the Government's policies, e.g. how to deal with crime.

D This person leads the Government and represents the nation in international affairs. He or she chooses the members of the Cabinet and other Gsovernment ministers. This person is the head of the armed forces and appoints senior judges.

I They are elected by the people who live in a particular area (constituency) in the town or country. They take their seats in the House of Commons. They discuss and vote on new laws.

C The monarch meets leaders from other countries, opens and closes Parliament and gives the royal assent to laws. The king or queen has no real power and takes little part in government.

E This is formed by the party with the second largest number of MPs in the House of Commons. Its job is to look carefully at the work of the Government and to challenge it if it thinks the Government is doing things that are not good for the country.

A There are two houses – the House of Commons and the House of Lords. The House of Commons makes laws and discusses important issues. Both houses look critically at the way the Government is doing its job.

B They help ministers run government departments and carry out the Government's policies. For instance, if the Government decides to build more hospitals, they ensure it is done. There are thousands of them working at different levels of importance.

F This is formed by the political party that wins the general election and has the most MPs in the House of Commons. It runs the country. The leader of this party becomes the Prime Minister.

H The voters are British people over eighteen years old who have the right to vote in elections. Members of the House of Lords, mental patients in institutions and prisoners serving sentences over twelve months are not allowed to vote.

DISCUSS

1 Is there anything about the way the Government works that surprises you?
2 Why do you think a large part of the system is designed to 'check' what the Government is doing?

You're in the Cabinet!

The Cabinet is the top government committee. It meets regularly and is chaired by the Prime Minister. Its members have to agree to support the policies the government decides to adopt. This is called collective responsibility – all of them are responsible for the Government's actions.

There are usually between 20 and 22 members in the Cabinet. You can see some of the key members and the main things they are responsible for in the illustration below.

Unfortunately, there is never enough money to pay for all the things the Government wants to do. If one department wants more money another has to lose it. The ministers have to argue in the Cabinet for the money they need for their departments.

Activity

1 Form small groups of four or five. You are mini cabinets. The Prime Minister has announced that government spending has to be cut and there is less money to go around. Seven ministers are arguing for more money for their departments. But others are arguing against them.
   a) Match the statements A–F with the ministers in the illustration who you think they fit best.
   b) Then match each statement A–F with one of the opposing arguments 1–7 on page 60.

Minister for Transport responsible for roads, railways and air travel and safety

Foreign Secretary speaks for the UK in its dealings with other countries

Minister for Welfare and Employment responsible for benefits of all kinds and pensions

Minister for Defence responsible for the defence of the country and the armed forces

Minister for Children and Education responsible for education and child protection

Prime Minister responsible for running the Government

Minister for the Environment responsible for looking after the environment, climate change measures and reducing pollution

A I desperately need a bigger share of the money available for building new hospitals and training a thousand more nurses. We need new scanning equipment that will spot brain diseases earlier and save hundreds of lives.

B We have to build more roads for the increasing amount of traffic. The railways also need more investment in high speed lines.

C The cost of security is rising all the time because of terrorist threats. We need more police and secret service agents. Reports have shown that our prisons are in a poor state. Millions of pounds need to be spent on them.

D We need more and better trained social workers to keep children safe. Many schools need to be improved by investing in buildings, equipment and more teachers.

E Time is running out for the environment with climate change accelerating. We have to build green sources of energy (using wind and wave power). We must support energy saving in homes.

F Our armed forces are committed all over the world. We need much better equipment to protect our troops and new weapons like tanks. The navy want to build a new aircraft carrier and the air force need new planes.

G Unemployment is rising so we will need to pay more unemployment benefit. We also need to spend more money on re-training people so they can find new jobs. Other benefits such as housing and disability allowances have to be increased in line with inflation.

Home Secretary
responsible for running the police force and the prisons, law and order and the justice system

Minister for Health
responsible for the National Health Service (NHS) and its hospitals, doctors and nurses and people's health

Chancellor of the Exchequer
responsible for managing the finances of the Government – how much is spent and how much is collected in taxes – and for preparing the budget

Activity

2 Because of the cuts, only four of the ministers can get more money, three will have to lose out. Your task is to decide which four win and which three lose. Everybody in your group has to agree your final choice and take responsibility for the decisions as a cabinet would. You have to be able to give good reasons why you chose to give money to some and not other departments.

Opposing arguments

1 *You use the excuse of terrorism all the time. We've got thousands of extra police officers, we don't need more. Prisons will just have to wait. After all prisoners committed the crimes and many people think life in prison is too comfortable as it is.*

2 *It is time we cut our commitments in other countries and stopped fighting in wars. We are not a major power anymore. We should spend money on things at home.*

3 *You can't keep on pumping money into the NHS forever, it just disappears. We could save money by cutting down on wastage in hospitals. Also we could stop some treatments and make people pay more for the medicines they receive.*

4 *If we build more roads, then the traffic will simply grow to fill them and it's bad for the environment. Railway passengers will have to pay for the new lines by paying higher fares.*

5 *Millions of pounds have gone into education and yet results have not significantly improved. It is changing the nature of education that will raise standards, not lots of money. We don't need to increase the spending this year.*

6 *We should root out benefits cheats before we pour more money in. We can't afford to increase unemployment benefit, so I'm afraid people will have to survive on existing payments or even lower ones.*

7 *The environment is not in such a bad state that it can't wait a little longer. We have more pressing needs now where we should be spending our money. Also it is not really clear how much benefit we get from some of these climate-saving measures.*

Paying for it!

The main way for the government to get money to pay for all it wants to do is by raising taxes. You can see the main taxes opposite. But people don't like having to pay more in taxes. And if the government makes them pay too much, it might lose the next general election.

Activity

You are the Chancellor of the Exchequer and you need to raise money to pay for your spending. Working in threes, decide which two taxes you would choose to increase. Explain why you chose these taxes rather than others.

Budget
Every year the Chancellor of the Exchequer has to produce a budget in which the government shows what it is spending and how it intends to tax people. Opposition parties look very critically at this and challenge anything they think is not a sensible thing to do. The budget directly affects all the people in the UK.

Think how your tax choices might affect:

- A family of two adults (both working) and three children who have an above average income who need to repair their house, travel a long way to work, smoke and drink.

- A single mother who lives on benefits and finds it hard to afford things.

- A businesswoman who employs eight people and her business is not doing too well. She is well off and spends a lot on a range of goods.

- A single male IT manager earning a high income who spends freely on cars, gadgets, consumer goods and entertainment.

There are two main types of tax

Direct tax

Income tax
This is a tax on the money you earn. It is called a progressive tax, because the more people earn, the more tax they pay.

National Insurance
This is a fixed percentage taken from what people earn to pay towards the National Health Service and social security benefits in case they become unemployed.

Corporation tax
Companies pay a percentage of their profits to the Government.

Indirect tax

This is a tax on the goods and services that people buy. Everybody pays the same amount of tax.

Customs and Excise duties
Payable on goods like petrol, alcohol, cigarettes and new cars.

VAT
Value Added Tax is paid on goods (e.g. computers, furniture) and services (e.g. building work). It is a percentage of the price, usually between 15 per cent and 20 per cent).

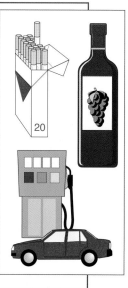

Which do you think is the fairest way of raising money – direct or indirect taxes?

Monarchy (being ruled by a king or queen) is one of the oldest forms of government. Traditionally, monarchs claimed that their right to rule had been given them by God. This was known as the Divine Right of Kings. Most countries in the world have got rid of their monarchies and become republics. Some, like Britain have become constitutional monarchies where the monarchs have given up most of their power to parliaments elected by the people.

B

What role does the monarch play?

The monarch is the third element in our parliamentary system. He or she is the 'head of state' and has a number of jobs. The monarch:

- opens and closes Parliament
- gives the royal assent to new laws
- after an election, asks the party that has the most MPs to form a government
- meets leaders of other countries
- is the symbolic head of the Commonwealth
- hands out medals and honours.

The monarch is also a symbol of Great Britain and a figurehead for the nation.

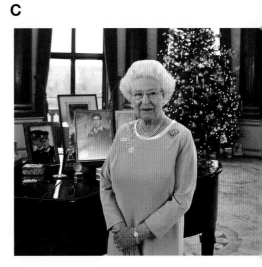

C

A

D

E

Activity

The photographs on pages 62–3 show the monarch playing different roles in our society and fulfilling different functions. Take each photograph in turn and either:

a) describe the role of the monarch, or
b) explain how she is a symbol or figurehead.
Refer to the list on page 62 to help you.

F

G

I

H

J

Is it time to get rid of the monarchy?

The future of the monarchy in our society is an important issue to debate as we move further into the twenty-first century. Some people would like to keep it as it is, others would like to see Britain become a republic. Some would like to keep the monarchy but change its role in a modern society. You are going to debate this. Before you do so, read pages 66–7: Developing your arguing skills.

Activity

Divide the class up into three main groups with smaller groups within each one. The three groups take one of these positions:

1 Keep the monarchy as it is.
2 Get rid of the monarchy and make Britain a republic.
3 Change the monarchy.

Allow time for each group to prepare their arguments using some of the points suggested on pages 64–5. You can use any of these points but you might have to change them to fit your argument (i.e. turn them around to say the opposite).

You can also research more arguments on the internet.

Debate the motion: We can no longer accept the monarchy in its present form.

Money and the monarchy

> The monarchy brings a huge amount of money to this country through tourism. The royal palaces and the parades and ceremonies are a major tourist attraction.

> You say that the monarchy brings in money through tourism. But what you have conveniently left out is how much the monarchy costs taxpayers. Millions of pounds of our money goes to pay for the upkeep of the palaces, for royal trips and visits and for royal ceremonies and banquets.

> The monarch now pays taxes, so some of the money comes from them.

> We pay a fortune for the royal family. There are lots of members whom we don't really know much about.

> We could just keep the monarch and a few members of the royal family but not pay for all the others, and also cut down the amount of money we pay out by, for instance, reducing the number of palaces they have.

Democracy, power and the monarchy

" The monarchy is not democratic; nobody voted for them. It would be better to have a president who is elected to be head of state. "

" Actually, the monarchy is more popular than most politicians who are elected. If you had a vote, the majority of people would vote for them. "

" How do you know this? You've just made it up. What evidence do you have for saying most people would vote to keep the monarchy? "

" A president is often only elected by a minority of the electorate and cannot adequately speak for the people who did not vote for him or her. So, accident of birth is the best means of appointing a head of state. This person is on no particular political side and their allegiance is to all the people, not just those who voted for them. "

" Your argument is not logical. Most people elected the president, even if it's a minority of the electorate. And to jump to the idea that 'accident of birth' is better just does not make sense. "

" The monarchy acts as a symbol of national unity in difficult times such as war or disaster. Everybody can unite behind them whatever political party they support. The monarch is neutral and does not side with any political party. It gives our country stability. "

" I agree that people can unite behind the monarchy but there is no reason why the President or Prime Minister should not be just as unifying during war and other crises. This happens in other countries without a monarch. "

Fairness, equality and the monarchy

" A lot of unfairness in our society is due to us having a royal family. It creates a system where some people are seen as better than others – a class system. Why should we have lords and ladies who are supposed to be better than ordinary people? If we get rid of the monarchy then we could have a more equal society. "

" The system of honours with medals and knighthoods, given out by the monarch, creates problems. Most of the important honours go to the rich and powerful making them even more powerful. It's very unfair and ought to be stopped. "

" I completely disagree. The monarchy is central to our heritage and traditions. It is an important part of what makes us British. People like to see ceremonies and parades and our society would be poorer without them. Also people should be rewarded for their contribution to society by getting medals and other honours. "

Developing your arguing skills

To be an effective active citizen you need to be able to put your point of view across to other people. This means that you need to argue your case by giving reasons for your views. You need to make clear points and support these by providing evidence or further explanation. We call this 'reasoned argument'.

Counter argument

When you debate with others you have to learn the skill of responding to what people say and challenging their arguments. Sometimes this involves simply putting across the opposite point of view but a more effective way is to find things wrong with their argument. Below are four ways of doing this.

Example

Point
It is important to keep the monarchy because the king or queen can unify the country in difficult times.

Reason
The monarch does not side with any political party and does not get involved in political arguments. So in times of crisis the people of the UK can unite behind the monarch. This is particularly true in times of war or economic depression when people might lose trust in politicians or there might be disagreements between different political groups.

Activity

You can see examples of the four types of challenge in the arguments about the monarchy on the previous two pages. Find an example of each one.

1 Challenge the speaker directly. Ask the speaker to provide evidence for their views or challenge their evidence, Examples are:

- 'What evidence do you have for saying that?'
- 'I don't trust the source of your evidence, it's a biased source.'
- 'The figures I have contradict yours.'

2 Some arguments don't make sense – they are not logical. Point this out to the speaker. For example:

- 'There is something wrong with what you're saying. It does not make sense ...'

Challenging the arguments of others

3 Sometimes people leave out important bits of an argument. Point out what they are leaving out. For example:

- 'I do not think you have given us the full story. What you have not said is ...'

4 Accept part of the argument of your opponent but not all of it. For example:

- 'I agree with the first part of what you say, but not the rest of your argument.'

Speaking persuasively

There are a number of techniques to persuade people to agree with your viewpoint. Here are several:

- Use persuasive words such as surely, obviously, undoubtedly, e.g. 'it is undoubtedly the case that ...'.

- Use emotive words to create sympathy or affect emotions such as noble, tortured, cruel, wise, e.g. 'these animals were tortured in experiments ...?'.

- Make people feel guilty if they don't accept your argument or appeal to their better nature, e.g. 'could you stand by and watch the suffering caused by ...?'.

- Find an expert who supports your views, e.g. 'Professor Green, this country's leading authority says ...'.

- Suggest that it is a popular view, e.g. 'most people agree with me when I say ...'.

- Suggest that there is some sort of threat or danger, e.g. 'if we don't deal with knife crime now, it will not be safe for people to go out at night ...'.

- Make them believe there are only two options, your one or an unattractive one, e.g. 'you either give people the right to die or condemn them to live out the rest of their lives in great pain'.

Other tips

- Vary the tone of your voice and sometimes speak louder and sometimes softer. Don't go on monotonously in the same tone.

- Get your body language right. Stand upright, look straight ahead and look confident.

- Keep your audience's attention:
  - make eye contact
  - don't read directly from a book or sheet of paper
  - try to look only briefly at your notes and keep looking at the audience
  - use humour if you can or put in a little story.

Reflection

How well do you think you're doing?
Think back over the work you have done in Section 2.

Skills

- Draw a chart like the one below, and give yourself a grade from 1 to 5, where 1 is the lowest and 5 is the highest.
- Give evidence for your score and say how you could improve your skills.

How well can you ... ?	1	2	3	4	5	Evidence for your score?	How can you improve?
discuss different ideas							
listen to other people's views							
challenge the arguments of others							
argue and make a case for a point of view							
plan action to influence others							

Understanding

- What do you understand by the following?
  political party   manifesto   policy
- Complete these sentences:
  'The job of the House of Commons is ...'
  'The main job of the Prime Minister is to ...'
  'The Official Opposition is ...'
- Which organisations do these logos represent?

- What are pressure groups?
- Identify five ways in which you can get your views heard and influence people.
- Talk to another pupil and discuss what you think was the most important thing you learned in this section.

Clues for Activity from pages 62–3

A Opening Parliament
B On currency
C Giving an annual speech on TV
D Meeting a Head of State
E Awarding someone a Member of the Order of the British Empire (MBE) medal
F Ceremonial occasion
G Meeting World leaders
H Giving royal assent to a law
I Attending a Commonwealth event
J On a royal visit to a hospital

Britain and the world

It is very important that countries of the world work together to try to solve the problems that all human beings face. The problems include economic crisis, climate change, poverty in developing countries, overpopulation and terrorism. Countries also need to trade with each other, and agree rules for working together.

Britain has, for centuries, formed relationships with other countries, particularly those within the British Empire, and now the Commonwealth. We are also members of major world organisations such as the United Nations (UN) and we belong to the European Union (EU). Being a member of international organisations such as these gives our country a voice in decision-making, but some people believe that we can lose our independence.

How do we solve global problems?

How do global problems affect individuals?

What is the point of the Commonwealth?

What does the United Nations do?

What are the advantages and disadvantages of the European Union?

Map showing EU member states

Assessing your progress
In this section you will be assessing how well you can:

- express and explain views that may not be your own
- make a case for a viewpoint
- use presentation skills
- detect bias and 'spin' in newspaper reports
- research using the internet
- develop your understanding of global problems.

KEY WORDS

globalisation

sovereignty

interdependence

conflict resolution

United Nations

Commonwealth

European Union

Air travel, the internet, email and mobile technology have all led to people and companies moving around the world – for trade, for work, for a better life – and made the world more interdependent. However, the rapid rate of change in technology, transport and communication has created new difficulties for governments.

Although people can communicate better across the world, countries still disagree about who owns territory and about political and religious ideas. They also disagree about how to tackle the problems that affect everyone living on this planet. Some of the major problems are shown below.

A Economic crisis
Because of globalisation, economic problems in one country will affect others. Multi-national corporations operate in many countries and financial collapse in one country will lead to job losses and hardship for workers in other countries.

B Migration
Poorer nations are getting poorer because of inequalities between nations, drought, wars, and sometimes, corrupt governments. Debt prevents these countries being able to develop economically and to provide a good standard of living for their people, so many leave their homes for a better life. They become economic migrants to richer countries.

DISCUSS

1 Which of these problems do you think are the most serious? Put them in order of seriousness and explain why.
2 Are there any world problems not listed here that you think are just as serious as these?

C Terrorism
People can plan and co-ordinate terrorist acts for political purposes, using the internet, and move from one country to another very quickly using air travel. Aeroplanes have become a target for terrorists.

D Nuclear threat
The 'nuclear arms race' between the Superpowers (the USA and the USSR) in the second half of the twentieth century means that there are thousands of nuclear warheads in the world. More countries want to develop their own weapons, and there is a fear that one day nuclear weapons will be used in a real war.

E Climate change
The growth of industrialisation and transportation across the world has led to the increased use of fossil fuel energy which has contributed to climate change, with serious consequences for the human race.

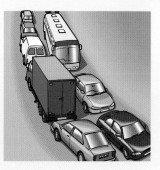

The world's problems cannot be solved by countries working alone. Governments need to get together to talk through problems and disagreements so that they all agree about the actions that need to be taken. There are different groupings of countries that meet to try to solve problems that affect them, for example, the Commonwealth, the African Union, the G8 and the G20.

The biggest economies in the world, together with the emerging economies, are called the G20.

Australia Brazil Canada China France

Argentina

Germany

A representative of the European Union

India

Indonesia

USA

Italy

United Kingdom

Japan

Turkey

Mexico

The leaders of these countries meet every year to discuss current problems

South Korea South Africa Saudi Arabia Russia

G20 STOP FOOLING ABOUT WITH OUR FUTURE

Activity

Research
Whenever the G20 meets, there are demonstrations by people who are frustrated by the lack of agreement on tackling world problems. Find out about the views of some of these groups, for example, Climate Camp, Rainbow Alliance, Stop the War Coalition or Third World Charities, and what they say the G20 should be doing. Make presentations of their different views.

Climate change

One of the most serious problems facing the world is climate change. For over 200 years people have been burning fossil fuels like coal and oil to provide energy for homes, factories and transport. When burned, they release carbon dioxide and other greenhouse gases into the atmosphere. Gases are also produced through waste pollution and intensive animal farming. These gases are said to contribute to warming the Earth. Scientists tell us that over the last 100 years, the Earth has warmed by 0.6 degrees Celsius. It may not sound a lot, but it has had some bad effects.

Melting ice from glaciers and the polar regions has led to rising sea levels, threatening coastal areas with flooding.

Sea water is becoming more acidic because of carbon dioxide dissolving in the water. This also has an effect on corals and sea life.

Warmer temperatures have led to heavier rainfall in some parts of the world, causing flooding. In other parts of the world, this has led to drought.

Hurricanes are becoming more frequent and are stronger.

Governments across the world have been trying to tackle the problem and to reduce the amount of carbon dioxide and other greenhouses gases from being produced. Some countries make good use of renewable energy sources, such as sun, wind, water, waves and biomass (plant and animal material), in order to generate electricity.

It is not easy to get agreement for all countries to reduce their carbon dioxide emissions when coal and oil are still such an important part of many countries' energy production. Countries such as China, India and South Korea say that they need to burn coal and oil to develop their economies.

The richer countries in the world have been burning fossil fuels for much longer than us, and caused most of the global warming.

We are producing goods that people all over the world want because they are cheap and good quality.

We need to continue to use fossil fuels to produce goods for our own people to give them a lifestyle and standard of living that people in the West take for granted.

Activity

1 How do you respond to these arguments from the emerging economies?
2 Work in small groups. Write an action plan for G20 leaders in which you explain the most important things richer countries could do to reduce emissions. Use the chart below to help you work out what you can include in your action plan. Make a copy of the chart. Some ideas have been put in for you but you can add others in all three columns. You have to take into account the obstacles or objections that might be put in the way of achieving your plan.

There are many things that governments could agree to do to encourage people to reduce emissions of greenhouse gases. Here are some suggestions. Can you think of others? Remember to identify possible obstacles or objections that might be raised and think about ways of overcoming these.

ACTION NEEDED	POSSIBLE OBSTACLES/ OBJECTIONS	WHAT GOVERNMENTS COULD DO
Increase use of wind, sun, water and wave power to generate electricity	People object to wind farms near their homes Still does not provide enough power for the country's needs	
Reduce use of aircraft		Tax aircraft fuel Raise air fares through extra taxes
Encourage people to drive cars less, use greener cars Use public transport		
Encourage less use of energy homes		Grants to householders for in insulation
Promote recycling which uses less energy and natural resources		

After the terrible destruction caused by the Second World War, European countries were anxious to prevent another war in Europe. In 1957, six countries signed the Treaty of Rome which founded the European Economic Community (EEC). The aim of this was to increase trade between them so that they could become more prosperous but also so they could become more closely connected with each other. The UK joined in 1973 because it could see the advantages of being part of a large trade group and did not want to be left out. There have been many changes since then. One of the biggest was in 1993 when the countries signed the Treaty of Maastricht which bound the countries together with a tighter set of rules. The EEC also changed its name to the European Union (EU).

The other big change in the EU over the years has been the number of countries that have joined. By 2010 this number had reached 27. However, other countries are still waiting to become part of the EU. These are known as candidate countries, such as Turkey.

The Treaty of Lisbon

This came into effect at the end of 2009 although it may take several years to put it into action. It marks a major step forward in giving more power to the EU. Some of the main points are as follows:

- A new President of the European Council who holds the office for two and half years.
- A High Representative for foreign affairs.
- The number of MEPs in the European Parliament will be fixed at 752.
- The European Parliament will be given more power to give it a greater say on how EU money is spent.
- In some areas countries will not be able to 'veto' decisions as they have done in the past.

Nobody knows how powerful the new President and High Representative for Foreign Affairs will be but they could play a big role on the world stage.

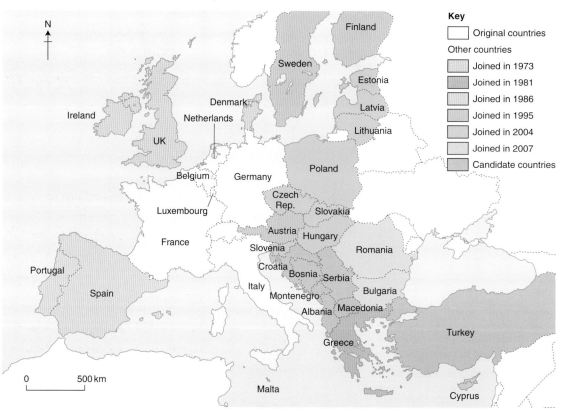

The Commission

The governments of the member countries choose commissioners to:
- carry out the day-to-day work of the EU
- propose and enforce new laws and regulations.

The Council of Ministers

Each member state sends one minister. Ministers:
- make key decisions
- discuss the proposals of the Commissioners and agree or disagree with them. If they disagree then the proposals may be changed or abandoned.

The main organisations of the European Union

The European Parliament

People in the member countries elect Members of the European Parliament (MEPs) who:
- meet in Brussels and Strasbourg
- debate and pass laws in conjunction with the Commission.

The European Court of Justice
- settles disputes between member countries
- gives rulings on European law.

Members of the European Parliament (MEPS)

Every five years elections are held where people can vote for the MEPs that represent the UK in the European Parliament. We need to know who they are and how we vote for them. The problem is that not many people in this country know who their MEPs are and what they do.

1 How are they elected?

There are twelve electoral regions in the UK with up to nine MEPs representing each region. In the election, UK citizens have one vote and vote for the party, e.g. Liberal Democrat, not a person. When the votes are counted up, the number of MEPs each party gets in that region depends on its share of the vote.

2 What do they do?

MEPs represent their region in the European parliament. They:
- work on new laws and debate issues affecting Europe
- check how the EU spends all the money it is given
- consult people about EU laws and regulations
- respond to you if you contact them.

Activity

Research

Work in threes.

1 a) Find out who your MEP is by contacting the UK Office of the European Parliament at www.euro parl.org.uk. Click on 'Your MEPS'.

   b) Find out who the MEPS are in your region and what political parties they belong to. Some have their own websites.

   c) Prepare two questions you wish to ask them about the EU or what they do.

   d) Choose the best five questions from the class and put them to the MEP.

2 You can find out more about the EU at www.europa.eu. Split the class up so that groups look at different aspects of the EU such as its history, more about the organisations above, the work of MEPs or current issues. Prepare brief presentations in which you tell the rest of the class about what you've found.

Advantages of the European Union

A The EU provides security for its members and greatly reduces the chances of a European war.

B Citizens of member states are able to travel to, migrate to, and live and work in the other member countries as a matter of right.

C EU regulations guarantee the standard of goods and protect consumers.

D The EU helps poorer member countries and regions to develop by giving them huge sums of money.

E The EU is a huge market of around 500 million people. Companies from one EU country find it easier to sell their goods and services in other EU countries because there are no barriers to trade. It helps companies to grow and Europe to be prosperous. Consumers get a wide choice of products.

F The EU has introduced strict rules on waste and pollution to protect the environment. It is bringing in measures to combat climate change.

G The EU can act as a big power bloc in relation to China and the USA and can have an impact on the world, for example in relation to climate change and aid to developing countries.

What do critics of the European Union say?

a The EU wastes a lot of money, especially on agricultural policies.

b The EU is undemocratic. Most of the decisions are made by people we don't know and can't question. Nobody knows who their MEP is and they don't have any power anyway.

c The UK has to pay an enormous amount of money to the EU which we could spend on other things.

d There are too many rules and regulations which restrict our lives and tie up our businesses in red tape. This makes it difficult for them to compete in the world and threatens jobs in the UK.

e EU organisations have too much power. Most laws are now made in Brussels. Our own government has lost the power to make laws and decisions about our economy and lots of things that affect our daily lives.

DISCUSS

1 Why do you think the candidate countries are anxious to join the European Union?
2 Choose the two advantages of being in the EU you would rank as most important.
3 Choose the two main criticisms you think are most significant. Explain your choices.

How does the EU affect us?

The European Parliament is responsible for passing many laws that affect the lives of all the inhabitants of the European Union. Over 70 per cent of the laws passed in our Parliament originate from the EU in Brussels: our Parliament puts them into British law. These laws affect, among other things, employment, health and safety, the environment, consumer rights, social security, and other aspects of everyday life.

Prison sentences for picking wild flowers under EU green laws

Dumping hazardous waste, polluting protected areas and collecting wild flowers would all be punishable by jail and hefty fines under new plans for EU-wide 'green crimes'. The drive by Brussels to extend its lawmaking powers into criminal areas was revealed by the leak of a draft directive listing a string of offences.

Daily Mail, 7 February 2007

EU ban on knobbly fruit and veg to be 're-peeled'

Knobbly carrots and curvy cucumbers will return to supermarket shelves from next summer when unpopular EU laws are scrapped. Imperfect fruit and vegetables are currently banned as EU marketing standards dictate that only the finest looking produce can be sold. But in a bid to make our greens cheaper as the cost of living rises, eurocrats argue it is time to lift the restrictions to prevent tonnes of edible produce going to waste every year.

Daily Express, 12 November 2008

Other EU directives

Here are just a few examples of other laws and 'directives' that have been passed by the European Parliament:

- The rights of passengers – transport operators must compensate passengers for delays. It also says that ticket prices must clearly show all charges and taxes that passengers must pay.
- Cheaper phone calls – a cap on the amount mobile phone companies can charge for calls and texts made and received abroad.
- Cleaner beaches – new standards on the cleanliness of beaches and water in rivers and lakes to reduce the likelihood of infections from bacteria.

Activity

1 Look at the newspaper extracts below.
   a) Identify the way EU rules and regulations affect us.
   b) Do you think what the EU is doing is helpful or unnecessary?
   c) Look at the panel below on other EU directives. Do you think these would be beneficial to UK citizens or not?
2 What do these extracts and directives tell us about the advantages and disadvantages of being in the EU?

Headlights on in day, says EU

British motorists are to be forced to drive with their headlights on during daytime under new EU laws. Ministers admitted yesterday they were losing a battle to opt out of the proposed rules. Eurocrats want all member states to follow Scandinavia, where dipped headlights are compulsory on all moving vehicles 24 hours a day. They say it would slash the number of accidents by making traffic more visible. But motoring groups warn it would boost fuel consumption and exhaust emissions by 3 per cent. And bikers who currently use their lights to stand out in daylight say they would lose the benefit if all cars did the same.

The Sun, 11 October 2006

How do we see the EU?

We don't always get to hear what the European Parliament has decided, since we rely on newspapers, television and radio for this kind of information. When newspapers do report on the European Union, they often choose the topics they think will interest their readers.

All newspapers have an 'editorial policy' on items in the news. This means that journalists will write stories that agree with the views taken by the editor. Sometimes the owner of the newspaper also influences this policy. The way a story is written to agree with a particular viewpoint is sometimes called 'spin'. You can usually work out what the editorial policy is by looking at the words used in an article.

Activity

1 What line does the newspaper article opposite take on the EU regulations about dogs in kitchens? How can you tell?

2 What is your opinion on the issue of dogs in B&B kitchens? Is the EU right?

3 Now look at all the newspaper extracts on pages 77 and 79.

   a) What spin is the newspaper putting on the story in each example (what does it want you to think about the EU)?

   b) Can you decide on the editorial policy of each of the newspapers towards the EU (is it for or against the EU)? What clues did you use?

4 Work in small groups of three or four. Research each of the 'directives' mentioned on page 77 in order to write a newspaper article.

   a) Decide on the editorial policy of your newspaper. Will you be for or against the EU?

   b) Now write a headline and a short paragraph about each of these EU directives, making sure that the story fits your editorial policy.

5 Find other examples of headlines and reports about the EU and decide whether the newspaper is for or against the EU.

DISCUSS

Where do you think we get our attitudes about the EU from? In many other EU countries, they are more interested and more positive about the EU.

EU bans pet from farm B&B

Farmhouse bed and breakfasts are under threat of closure because of an EU ruling which bans pet dogs from their owners' kitchens. Farmers say the sight of the family dog lounging by the Aga at breakfast time adds to the rustic charm for visitors. But according to officials the animal poses a potential health and safety hazard to guests' food. So health inspectors are using new EU food hygiene laws ... to have pets banned from kitchens. Tourism bosses fear that because most farmers only run B&Bs as a side business, many will close rather than exclude their pets. The ruling emerged after one B&B owner in Dorset had to give assurances to his local authority that his dog would not be in the kitchen at breakfast time.

> **❝ Many will close rather than exclude their pets. ❞**

David Weston, chairman of the British Bed and Breakfast Association, said he had never come across any previous case of food poisoning by dog hair. He added: 'This new law covers food businesses and because a bed and breakfast serves food, they fall into that category. The regulations weren't designed to cover people's homes, which is essentially what a bed and breakfast is. Most of our members practise good standards of cleanliness anyway. We think the regulations should be enforced in a commonsense way. When there is a dog in the corner of the room and nowhere near the food surface area, then we don't feel that is a threat or a danger to health.'

Trish Bowditch, 51, and husband Robert diversified into the B&B business five years ago after their children moved out of the farmhouse. They have a labrador, Maisie, who guests routinely make a fuss over at the Parnham Farm B&B near Bridport, Dorset. Mrs Bowditch said she would probably close if it came to it. She added: 'Maisie's home is in the kitchen by the Aga. We haven't got a suitable outhouse for her. I am always very particular when it comes to preparing food and I am extra careful to keep her away. She wanders around the dining area, but I always make sure the guests are okay with her first. Guests often ask if they can take her out for a walk. Maisie is part of the way we live and is a member of the household.'

> **❝ The world has gone barking mad. ❞**

Oliver Letwin, Tory MP for West Dorset, said: 'My conclusion is that this particular aspect of the world has gone barking mad.' But Will John, the principal environmental health officer at West Dorset District Council, said: 'Most people would agree it is not hygienic to have animals in kitchens where food is being prepared. A bed and breakfast may be somebody's home, but once a room is used to prepare high-risk food that is going to be sold to members of the public, it takes on a different meaning.'

Daily Mail, 12 June 2008

Who's the boss?

One of the biggest issues about the EU is how much political control it has over the lives of people in member countries. Many people are happy with some sort of economic union where we can trade freely with each other and have the benefits of a huge market. But some are not so keen on the way the EU makes all sorts of decisions which affect our daily lives. It is a question of sovereignty – in the case of the UK, should Parliament be the sovereign power or should the EU make the major decisions?

Activity

1 Decide whether you think the EU or the UK Government in Westminster should make decisions about the areas on pages 80–1, and be ready to justify your answer. Think about what you have already learned from pages 77–9 before you begin. Put your answers in one of three columns:

Should be decided by the UK Government	Should be decided by the EU	Not sure/it depends

1 Setting targets to lessen the impact of climate change (e.g. more wind and solar power). Also targets for air pollution.

2 The use of pesticides on food crops. This includes the type and strength of pesticides allowed to be used.

3 Control of the army, navy and air force – should they be part of a European defence force or under UK government control?

4 Measures to control the pollution of rivers and the quality of beaches at the seaside.

5 The prices fishermen and farmers should charge for their products.

6 The quality and standards of electrical goods.

7 The taxes that people pay – direct taxes like income tax as well as indirect taxes like the taxes on goods (e.g. petrol and alcohol).

8 The pensions that people receive and at what age they receive a pension.

9 How long we should work during the day and the number of days' holiday we are entitled to each year.

The euro

In 2002, twelve EU countries gave up their currencies and all now use the euro. They felt that it would be easier to trade, work and travel in the EU and would help their economies grow. It would help consumers because they would be able to compare the value of goods throughout the eurozone and get the best value. Critics say that joining the euro would mean the UK losing control of its own economic affairs.

10 The level of migration into the UK – the number of people allowed into the country.

11 How the courts and the system of justice works.

12 The protection of fish stocks in the seas around Britain.

13 The level of social security benefits, such as housing and unemployment benefit, paid to people in the UK.

14 The length of maternity leave and paternity leave allowed after a baby is born.

Activity

2 Look at the statements on pages 80–1. For each one, decide where along the continuum line your position would be.

a) Do you want the main decisions about the way we live to be taken ...

1	2	3	4	5

only by the UK government   mainly by the EU?

b) Do you feel that EU laws, rules and regulations:

1	2	3	4	5

are a huge burden on the UK and damage our way of life   make the UK a fairer and more equal place?

c) We should:

1	2	3	4	5

always keep the pound sterling as our currency   join the Euro if it is to our economic advantage

3 Compare your rankings with other members of the class and debate:
a) whether you think Britain should get more or less involved in Europe
b) how far you want EU laws and regulations to control aspects of life in Britain.

Britain occupies an important position in the Commonwealth. When Britain had a huge empire in the nineteenth century, it controlled a number of 'colonies' around the world. The English language along with British systems of law, administration and education were exported to these colonies. In the second part of the twentieth century, Britain's former colonies gained their independence. But many of them wanted to continue their relationship with Britain and with one another because they shared so much in common. Today the Commonwealth is a voluntary organisation of 54 independent countries with over two billion people. Queen Elizabeth II is its symbolic head.

In 1949, the modern Commonwealth was created and in 2009 it celebrated its 60th anniversary

What does the Commonwealth do?

- It provides advice on economic development to the smaller and least developed countries to help them improve the quality of life in each country and overcome poverty.
- It encourages democracy, helping to establish and build multi-party democracies, e.g. the Maldives in 2008, and sending groups to observe elections.
- It encourages member states to protect and manage their natural resources and support sustainable development, e.g. by agreements to protect fish stocks in the Pacific and conserving rainforests in Guyana.
- It helps countries establish human rights organisations. It has trained police oficers from forces across the Commonwealth to ensure that the human rights are protected.
- It promotes and supports many aspects of education, including teacher training and school inspection, helping countries to share ideas, particularly on educating the most disadvantaged groups.

What does the Commonwealth stand for?

The Harare Declaration of 1991 set out the Commonwealth's guiding principles, including:
- human dignity and equal rights for all citizens
- opposition to all forms of racism, racial prejudice and intolerance
- the rule of law
- the right to participate in free and democratic political processes.

How does the Commonwealth affect young people?

The Commonwealth has a special focus on young people in order to champion their rights and help them achieve their aims and ambitions. It has a number of programmes to help them escape illiteracy and poverty through:
- education and training
- sports, cultural and artistic pursuits
- enterprise projects.

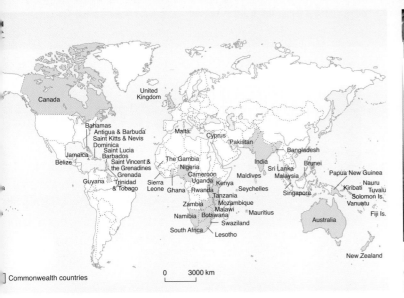

Commonwealth countries   0   3000 km

Every four years the Commonwealth Games is held in a different country. They are often called the 'friendly games' because of the goodwill between all those taking part

Does the Commonwealth have any real influence?

Critics of the Commonwealth say it has no real power because it has no direct influence over its members. However, member countries are committed to the guiding principles of the Commonwealth and this gives it moral authority, its main strength. The Commonwealth can suspend members who violate its principles to show the wider world that it disapproves of their actions.

1   It mounted a strong campaign against apartheid and racial discrimination in South Africa. South African goods were boycotted in some countries and there was a ban against playing South African whites-only teams.

2   In 1995 it suspended Nigeria's membership after the military seized power and executed the writer Ken Saro-Wiwa and other activists who objected to this.

3   Pakistan has been suspended several times when military governments have taken over and re-admitted when democratic government was re-established.

4   In 2002, Zimbabwe was suspended after President Robert Mugabe used violence and intimidation during elections and put opposition politicians in jail. Later, Zimbabwe pulled out of the Commonwealth.

5   In 2009, Fiji was suspended because it refused to hold democratic elections. Its present leader seized power in a coup in 2006. It is not allowed to attend Commonwealth meetings or the Commonwealth Games in 2010 or receive economic and technical aid.

DISCUSS

1 Which guiding principles of the Commonwealth did the countries listed on the left break?
2 What do you think is the value of the Commonwealth Games for athletes and their countries?
3 In your opinion, what is the point of the Commonwealth?

Activity

Research
Research current issues and the work of the Commonwealth at www.thecommonwealth.org. Find out about the projects it has set up for young people.

The United Nations aims to prevent wars, solve problems between countries, resolve conflict and promote human rights and freedoms for all the people of the world. It's a big task and unsurprisingly the UN is often not successful in achieving its aims. Britain has always played an important role in the UN and is a member of the Security Council.

Activity

1 Look at the photographs below and work out some of the things the UN does. The page opposite will help you do this.

How did the UN begin?

The United Nations was set up in 1945 when 51 nations signed its charter. The world had just come through a horrendous war and world leaders wanted to find ways of countries settling disputes peacefully.

They also wanted to build a better world and in 1948 signed the Universal Declaration of Human Rights. It set up agencies to promote education, health, workers' rights and deal with crises and disasters.

General Assembly

All member states send a representative to the General Assembly to discuss world issues. Each country has one vote on UN resolutions. However, the General Assembly can only make recommendations; countries do not have to go along with what it decides.

The Security Council

There are five permanent members of the Security Council – Russia, China, Britain, France and the USA – and ten other countries who join it for shorter periods. This Council makes the most important decisions about areas of conflict in the world, such as to send in a peacekeeping force.

How is the UN organised?

Secretary General

He or she is the spokesperson of the UN and plays a role in world affairs. The Secretary General is the head of the Secretariat, the staff who run the UN.

International Court of Justice

Based at The Hague in Holland, it settles legal disputes between countries. It also runs the War Crimes Commission.

Some UN Agencies

- **The World Health Organisation (WHO)** tries to improve health around the world. For instance, it runs immunisation programmes and tries to combat pandemics.
- **The United Nations High Commission for Refugees (UNHCR)** draws up plans and co-ordinates action to help refugees.
- **The International Labour Organisation (ILO)** seeks to improve the rights and conditions of workers around the world.
- **The United Nations Children's Fund (UNICEF)** works to support children by ensuring they have clean water, food to eat, health care and education. It also tries to keep families together in times of crisis or disaster.

Activity

2 Split up the class into small groups and research UN Agencies. Find out:

- what they do
- where they work
- examples of projects/programmes they have carried out
- any other interesting information about them.

Many have their own websites or you can start from the main United Nations website www.un.org.
Each group can take a different agency and report back their findings to the rest of the class.

DISCUSS

What is the point of the United Nations?

One of the main roles of the United Nations is to prevent wars and try to resolve conflicts and make peace. It also arranges ceasefires and sends in peacekeeping forces to keep warring sides apart. Sometimes these wars are between countries but often they are between different groups within a country. The UN has had successes such as the Korean War (1950–55), preventing the Communist takeover of South Korea, and the First Gulf War (1990–91), overturning the invasion of Kuwait by Iraq, and arranging ceasefires as in the Iran-Iraq war in 1988. It has for many years had a peacekeeping force in Cyprus keeping the Greeks and the Turks apart.

UN armoured personnel carriers, Sarajevo, Bosnia

Sudanese refugees at Bahai UNHCR refugee camp, Chad

A What are the causes of conflict?

- Arguments over land.
- Arguments between different races or ethnic groups.
- Religious differences.
- Disputes about resources, like water and oil.
- People being oppressed, e.g. not allowed to vote.
- Desire to control and dominate others – power.

However, it also has had failures when it has been unable to sort out desperate situations, such as Bosnia in the 1990s, Israel and Palestine over the last 60 years and Darfur in the first decade of the twenty-first century. Critics say that it is ineffective and lacks teeth: it has not done well on preventing wars.

The problem for the UN and the world in general is that it is very hard to resolve conflicts which often have deep-seated causes (see panel A). There are also reasons why it is sometimes difficult for the UN to step in and help the two sides resolve their differences (see panel B).

B Why can't the UN sort out these conflicts easily?

- Member countries don't agree on what should be done.
- Some countries don't support human rights and don't always see the need to intervene in cases where human rights are the central issue.
- The big powers, particularly the USA, China and Russia, have different political aims and ambitions. They often won't co-operate.
- It can be difficult to get the money to pay for UN operations.
- If you are trying to make peace between two sides, they have to be willing to stop fighting.

Activity

Working in small groups:

1 Suggest examples for each of the causes of conflict listed in panel A. These could be international (between countries), national (between different groups within a country) or local to your area. They can be from the present or from the past.

2 Identify the main reasons, suggested by panels B and C, why it is difficult for the UN to keep peace and resolve conflicts.

3 Why do you think conflicts often get a lot worse before they get better?

4 What do you think has to take place first before groups can come to the table to resolve their differences?

5 Discuss your answers with the whole class.

C Why do attempts to resolve conflict break down?

- The differences of ideas (religious, political or ethnic) are so strong that nothing can stop the violence.

- People want revenge for things done to them.

- People want justice and want people who have committed evil deeds to be punished.

- Fear of the other side.

- One or both of the sides feel that things have not been sorted out fairly and/or they have had things forced on them.

Resolving conflicts

Even when countries or groups come together to resolve their problems it is not easy to reach agreement and end the conflict. You can see some of the main reasons for this in panel C. However, reconciliation can be brought to situations that seem almost impossible to resolve. This is often done through a process of conflict resolution which uses the techniques or principles shown below.

Some principles of conflict resolution

1 Establish exactly what the two sides are fighting about.

2 Focus on the problem, not the people, going over what one side has done to the other. Both sides need to co-operate against the problem.

3 Establish the shared concerns and needs of both sides. Focus on what both sides want to get out of the situation.

4 Work on active listening rather than passive hearing. Things get worse if both sides try to talk rather than listen, trying to think about what they are going to say next rather than really listening to what the other person is saying.

5 Choose a neutral place to meet, away from the place of conflict.

6 Use an outside mediator, respected by both sides, to help with negotiations.

7 Start with what is do-able rather than trying to sort out everything. Making peace can take a long time and might need to start with small steps.

8 Both sides have to be prepared to compromise.

9 The solution has to be practical and seen to be fair to both sides.

10 Both sides need to be able to forgive each other to some extent rather than focus on vengeance.

Activity

On pages 88–90 are three case studies of serious and long-running conflicts. Two have been resolved to some degree and one has proved intractable (difficult to resolve) over many years.

1 Make a copy of the chart opposite and complete it as you read the first two case studies about South Africa and Northern Ireland.

2 What is the current situation in these two countries? Have all the problems been resolved?

	South Africa	Northern Ireland
What were the causes of the conflict?		
Why was it hard to resolve it (use panel C)?		
What key principles of conflict resolution were used?		
What other factors allowed peace to be made, even ones that seem unfair and unjust?		

Case Study 1: South Africa

For the greater part of the twentieth century the South African government pursued a policy of apartheid, the separation of whites and blacks. In reality, this meant that the whites controlled all the wealth and power, based on the exploitation of black people. Black people were denied their human rights and civil liberties. Whites enforced their domination by brutality, violence and torture. Nelson Mandela of the African National Congress led a campaign of resistance for which he was imprisoned in 1962. He remained in jail for the next 27 years. However, by the 1990s the South African government could no longer withstand the pressure of world opinion and talks began to resolve the conflict. Key factors in this were:

- The leaders of both sides were prepared to talk, led on the South African side by F.W. de Klerk.
- Nelson Mandela was released and urged black South Africans not to seek revenge through violence.
- Mandela became an inspirational leader who was able to speak to whites as well as blacks and heal the rifts between them.

- A Truth and Reconciliation Committee was set up. Whites who had committed acts of violence, murder and torture were not prosecuted if they attended the TRC and told the truth about what had happened. Many showed remorse for what they had done and it helped people to come to terms with the horrors of apartheid.

Case Study 2: Northern Ireland

In 1922 Ireland was divided into the Irish Free State (EIRE) and Northern Ireland, under the control of the British government. But many Irish nationalists, supported by their armed wing, the Irish Republican Army (IRA), passionately wanted to see a united Ireland. However, in Northern Ireland the Unionists were just as passionate about remaining part of the UK. What made this matter more complicated was that the Unionists were largely Protestant and the Nationalists were largely Catholic, so it was a religious as well as a political conflict. The Protestant Unionists were in the majority in Northern Ireland and controlled the region. The Catholic minority felt they were being badly treated and subject to discrimination in areas like jobs and housing. Trouble erupted in the 1970s when the Catholics in Northern Ireland demanded equal civil rights. The British army was brought in and the situation escalated. It led to horrific violence, killings, assassinations and bombings in Ireland and on the UK mainland. But by the 1990s the two sides were ready to resolve their conflict. Key factors in this were:

- The people of Northern Ireland wanted the violence to end.

- All sides could see that the killings and bombings were not going to achieve what they wanted.
- Key people, including leading politicians and church leaders on both sides started talking.
- An outside mediator, George Mitchell, an American senator, was brought in who was respected by both sides. This led to the Good Friday agreement in 1998 which brokered peace between the two sides. In a referendum the people supported the agreement.
- The IRA and Unionist paramilitaries were prepared to decommission their weapons, an essential demand before there could be a final settlement.
- Prisoners were released to ensure good faith even though some had committed murders.

Activity

3 Read Case Study 3 on page 90 and identify the factors that have made this situation so difficult to resolve. Use panel C from page 87 to help you.

4 When you have finished reading this whole section, consider the nine factors opposite. Arrange them in the shape of a diamond, putting the one you think most important in resolving conflicts at the top, the next two in the next row, and so on (see diagram). Give reasons for your answers and discuss with the whole class.

- Face-to-face meetings between both sides
- Interaction between people on both sides so they get to know each other better
- Outside mediators
- UN resolutions and UN peacekeepers
- Involvement of other governments
- Willingness to forgive each other and not seek revenge
- Willingness to make peace and end the conflict
- Amnesty for people who have committed terrible acts on both sides
- Inspirational leaders.

Case Study 3: Arab/Israeli conflict

In 1947, the United Nations voted to divide Palestine up into Jewish and Arab (Palestinian) controlled areas, establishing the state of Israel. The Palestinians and surrounding Arab countries rejected this and launched a war against the Jews (Israelis). The Israelis won and also defeated the Arabs in 1966 and 1973. As a result they ended up controlling a large part of Palestine. Since then, more and more Jewish settlers have settled on Palestinian land. The Palestinians regard this as the occupation of their land and have mounted a ferocious terrorist campaign carried out by the Palestinian Liberation Organisation (PLO) and Hamas, including rocket attacks and suicide bombings. The Israelis have retaliated by sending in their military forces to crush the Palestinians. They have also built a huge wall to separate off Jewish controlled areas from Palestinian land. There have been many attempts to resolve this conflict. UN peacekeeping forces have been used and in the 1990s agreement was very nearly reached using outside mediators. But extremists on both sides have driven the two sides apart and hatred between the two sides has grown in intensity.

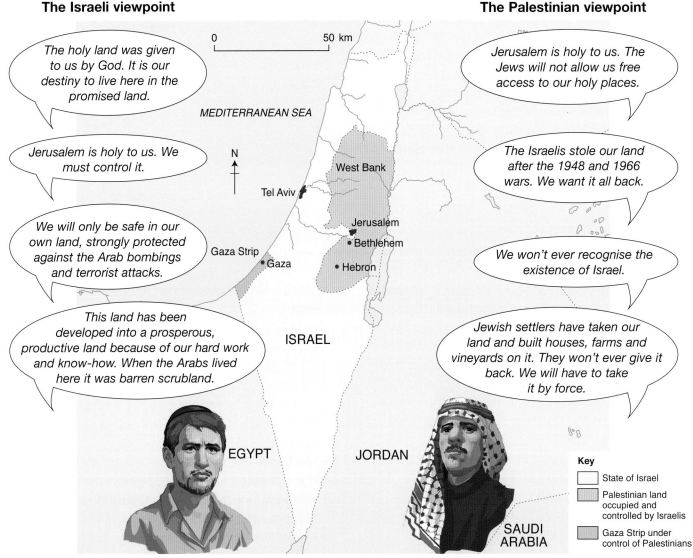

The Israeli viewpoint

The holy land was given to us by God. It is our destiny to live here in the promised land.

Jerusalem is holy to us. We must control it.

We will only be safe in our own land, strongly protected against the Arab bombings and terrorist attacks.

This land has been developed into a prosperous, productive land because of our hard work and know-how. When the Arabs lived here it was barren scrubland.

The Palestinian viewpoint

Jerusalem is holy to us. The Jews will not allow us free access to our holy places.

The Israelis stole our land after the 1948 and 1966 wars. We want it all back.

We won't ever recognise the existence of Israel.

Jewish settlers have taken our land and built houses, farms and vineyards on it. They won't ever give it back. We will have to take it by force.

0   50 km

MEDITERRANEAN SEA

N

West Bank

Tel Aviv

Jerusalem

Bethlehem

Gaza Strip

Gaza

Hebron

ISRAEL

EGYPT

JORDAN

SAUDI ARABIA

Key

State of Israel

Palestinian land occupied and controlled by Israelis

Gaza Strip under control of Palestinians

Note: These are simplified views of what is a very complex issue

Developing your mediation skills

Disagreement is not confined to countries. There are often disagreements between individuals, which cause a lot of distress to those people involved. Every day people fall out: couples, families, neighbours, work colleagues and friends. The principles of conflict resolution are similar for these people as for whole countries.

Here are some of the causes of conflict between individuals:

- An accusation of theft has been made.
- Money is owed and has not yet been repaid.
- Someone has said that people have been talking behind a person's back.
- A boyfriend/girlfriend has gone off with someone else.

Activity

1 Look at the box above. Add at least four more common causes of conflict between individuals.
2 Work in groups of three. Look at the arguments on both sides in the examples below. Role-play each of these situations, with two people taking on points of view A and B and the third person being the mediator. The mediator must use the principles of conflict resolution on page 87.
3 See whether you can come to an agreement within ten minutes for each situation.
4 In your threes, try role-playing several more of the conflicts from your list.
5 Join up with another group of three at the end of the role-plays and discuss what works and what doesn't when trying to resolve conflict.

Neighbours disagree about the condition of a fence	
POINT OF VIEW A	**POINT OF VIEW B**
The fence is your responsibility.	The fence is your responsibility.
The fence is broken and ugly and should be repaired.	The fence is not too bad.
You should pay for the repairs.	The cost of repair would be more than I could afford.

Brothers/sisters disagree about who should inherit some property (e.g. a gold watch)	
POINT OF VIEW A	**POINT OF VIEW B**
The father said the watch should go to the eldest child, me.	No, the father promised the watch to me.
It's normal for the eldest to inherit family heirlooms.	You have already inherited other items.
None of the others wanted it.	I always liked the watch.

Reflection

How well do you think you're doing?
   Think back over the work you have done in Section 3.

Assessing your progress
In this section you will be
assessing how well you can:
* express and explain views
  that may not be your own
* make a case for a viewpoint
* use presentation skills
* detect 'spin' in newspaper
  reports
* research using the internet
* develop your understanding
  of global problems.

Skills

* Draw a chart like the one below, and give yourself a grade from 1 to 5, where 1 is the lowest and 5 is the highest.
* Give evidence for your score and say how you could improve your skills.

How well can you ... ?	1	2	3	4	5	Evidence for your score?	How can you improve?
express and explain your views							
make a case and debate your views with other people							
present your findings to other people							
detect spin in newspaper reports							
carry out research on the internet							

Understanding

* Identify five global problems.
* Choose two and say why it is necessary for countries to work together to solve them.
* Give two advantages and two disadvantages of the European Union.
* What are the main causes of conflict in the world?
* Why is it so difficult to resolve conflicts?
* Which organisations do the symbols below represent and what are their main purposes?

* Talk to another pupil and discuss what you think was the most important thing you learned in this section.

Glossary

active citizen someone who wants to change things for the better, who is prepared to argue for and take action to change things or resist an unwanted change.

ballot box where ballot papers are put.

ballot paper paper with the names of all the candidates who want to be elected. Voters choose one by putting a cross next to the appropriate name.

campaign the activities that candidates and their supporters undertake to persuade people to vote for them.

candidate person standing for election.

censorship banning or changing material (newspaper articles, books, films) to prevent it being seen by the public.

civil liberties the right to freedom of speech and action.

coalition government where two or more political parties form a government to run a country.

collective responsibility a whole group taking responsibility for the decisions its members make or the actions they take.

Commonwealth a voluntary organisation of 54 countries with the king or queen of the UK as its nominal head.

conflict resolution ways to lessen or eliminate conflict between people, groups or countries.

constituency the voters in a particular area who elect an MP to Parliament.

democracy a system of government where people regularly elect their leaders and have a say in the way a country is governed.

direct action action taken where the normal channels are regarded as too slow or ineffective, often some sort of disruptive activity, legal or illegal, to arouse public awareness or achieve an objective.

discrimination treating someone unfairly as a result of prejudice.

economic sanctions economic penalties imposed on a country – e.g. not trading with the country, boycotting some of its goods, refusing to sell the country particular goods – by other countries.

election a way of choosing someone for a particular position by voting.

electorate all the people who can vote in an election.

emerging economies economies, like China, India and Brazil which are growing fast and becoming more important in world trade and affairs.

equal opportunities having a fair chance, regardless of gender, race, religion or other beliefs, to receive an education, get a job and promotion, obtain housing, etc.

European Union an organisation of 27 European states which aims to maintain peace in Europe and develop economic and social policies that will benefit the people of Europe.

fossil fuels sources of energy which use coal and oil.

free countries countries which have democracies, where people have a say in government, and civil rights.

G20 the group of 20 (19 countries plus the European Union) – industrialised and emerging economics – whose representatives meet to discuss financial and economic matters which affect the whole world.

G8 a group of eight leading world economies – USA, France, UK, Germany, Russia, Japan, Canada and Italy who meet to discuss economic matters affecting the world.

globalisation the increasing connections between people, companies and countries around the world through new technologies and improved communications, particularly in respect of trade.

human rights rights that are held to belong to any person. The United Nations Universal Declaration of Human Rights, 1948, sets out a full list of the rights that all people should have. These include the right to life, liberty, education, freedom of movement and equality before the law.

hung parliament where no party has a clear majority and has to rely on the support of other parties to win votes in Parliament.

interdependence the way countries depend on each other, through trade, for their survival and well-being.

law a rule that has the backing of the Government.

manifesto a statement of policies and aims.

Parliament the place where people meet to discuss important issues, make laws and question the Government about the way it is running the country.

party manifesto a statement of the party's aims and policies.

policies courses of action that people plan to carry out or are in the process of carrying out.

political party an organised group of people who share a particular set of values, views and objectives and who put forward people to stand in elections.

polling station the place where the voters cast their votes, often a school or a church hall.

prejudice opinions that we form without knowing all the facts or much information.

pressure group an organisation that has strong opinions on a particular issue and attempts to influence the people who make decisions.

Proportional representation an electoral system in which the number of seats a party gets is in proportion to the number of votes it receives.

republic a system of government where the people or their elected representatives hold power rather than a monarch. Usually, the head of state is called the president.

Returning Officer the person who is in charge of counting the votes in a constituency and declares who the winner is after the count.

sovereignty the authority of a state to exercise power, to make laws and run its own affairs.

surveillance being watched; observing the behaviour of people especially by government organisations.

United Nations a world organisation, to which most of the countries of the world belong, which aims to prevent wars, resolve conflicts, solve world problems and promote human rights.

Index